'This book combines technical theory 'boo experience 'street smarts' in a flowing read can easily read cover-to-cover or dip into reference. It is applicable for all levels and functions within a company. At a high level, it enables an appreciation of the tasks and responsibilities of peers. At a detailed level, it provides practical examples to copy or to adapt into local work flows and processes to bring immediate benefits in understanding, process efficiency and subsequent increased margins.'

Mr Stephen Oliver, Vice President Marketing & Sales
Vicor Corporation, Boston, USA

'Bamford and Forrester have done an excellent job in creating a concise, salient, and appealing approach to explain the basics of Operations Management to students who desire a primer on the subject. They have captured the essential elements of designing processes, products and work organizations; exploring approaches to operations planning and control; managing change through effective project management and technology transfer; and then managing quality and improvement strategies.'

Professor Rob Handfield, PhD, Bank of America University Distinguished
Professor of Supply Chain Management, Consulting Editor, Journal of
Operations Management
Department of Business Management, College of Management, North
Carolina State University, USA

'This is an excellent concise text that introduces students to all of the key areas of operations management. It should be an invaluable aid for students in understanding all of the major aspects of operations and their importance to the success of businesses.'

ESSENTIAL GUIDE TO OPERATIONS MANAGEMENT

ESSENTIAL GUIDE TO OPERATIONS MANAGEMENT
Concepts and Case Notes

DAVID R. BAMFORD
PAUL L. FORRESTER

A John Wiley and Sons, Ltd., Publication

Registered office
John Wiley & Sons Ltd, The Atrium, Southern Gate, Chichester, West Sussex, PO19 8SQ, United Kingdom

For details of our global editorial offices, for customer services and for information about how to apply for permission to reuse the copyright material in this book please see our website at www.wiley.com.

Library of Congress Cataloging-in-Publication Data

Bamford, David R.
  Essential guide to operations management : concepts and case notes / by David R Bamford & Paul L Forrester.
    p. cm.
  Includes bibliographical references.
  ISBN 978-0-470-74949-4
  1. Production management. I. Forrester, Paul L., 1961- II. Title.
  TS155.B2476 2009
  658.5–dc22

                                                                2009037049

978-0-470-74949-4

A catalogue record for this book is available from the British Library.

Typeset in 11.5/15 Giovanni by Laserwords Private Limited, Chennai, India
Printed and bound in Great Britain by TJ International, Padstow, Cornwall

CONTENTS

1 OPERATIONS MANAGEMENT IN CONTEXT

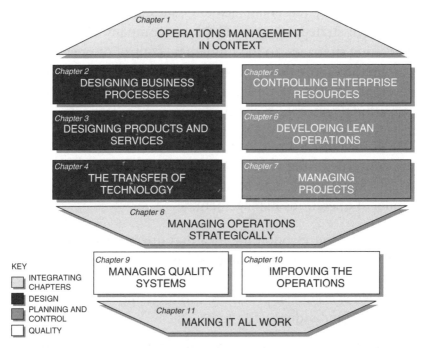

Conceptual model of operations management

Introduction

The aim of any service, public sector or retail or industrial operation is to deliver goods and services of the quality, quantity, cost and availability that will satisfy the customers' needs while at the same time making most effective use of resources. This can only be achieved by giving attention to the design of products, processes and work for employees, and through competent planning and control. This is what Operations Management is about. This book presents the fundamental principles of operations management in a novel and structured way that is appropriate to the needs of contemporary Operations Managers, and students in this field.

Operations management covers decision making in the organization, from top level management issues such as developing an operations strategy congruent with the company's business and marketing strategies, to the immediate control of operations. It is, therefore, more than operational management. Each chapter develops an understanding of the theory and practice of key operational concepts to enable delivery of the strategy.

The book is structured in a unique manner, to better reflect the concerns of the contemporary Operations Manager in the twenty-first century. The book is based around the conceptual model of operations management.

The model centres upon the idea that operations management comprises three essential components:

1. *Design of operations* processes, products and services, and the work of individuals;

2. *Planning and control* of operations once designs are in place and operational; and

3. Ensuring *quality* of products and services produced and delivered, and (wherever possible) improving on these.

However these cannot be addressed in isolation. The essential element in *effective* operations management is the *integration* of these components. The book therefore contains three integrating chapters:

1. We need to understand **operations management in context**. What is its purpose in a business sense? And how and where does it relate to the other business functions.

2. How might we **manage operations strategically**? Design, planning and control activities must not be conducted totally independently of one another, so we need the means to coordinate our activities within a formulated operations strategy. We believe that operations strategy is best covered not at the start or end of the text (as you find in most other operations management books), but in the middle, after the principles of design and operations planning and control are well understood.

3. We need to consider the implementation of the principles contained in this book, so we need to look at **making it all work** in the final chapter. Implementation is identified by practitioners as the most critical activity, but is often overlooked or skimmed over in texts, so we address this head-on in this book.

The conceptual model offers a comprehensive and up-to-date view of the operations management function and it can be seen that we have integrated contemporary topics such as technology transfer, project management and lean operations (often discussed and also critical in business, but often overlooked in any depth within existing texts). But, before embarking on these topics, it is important that we fully grasp and comprehend what the practice of operations management comprises, and also where it has evolved from in an historical and theoretical context.

Basic principles of operations systems performance

The task of the operations manager can be summarized at a basic level as converting a range of resource inputs, through the operations process, into a range of outputs in the form of products. However, the various elements that together make up this management function are diverse and complex in nature. The operations manager must have competencies in human resource management, strategic awareness, product knowledge, systems and organizational design and, at the operating level, of planning and control. Moreover, the task of the operations manager is often misunderstood and is often relegated to a reactive rather than a positive and proactive role within the organization. To indicate the importance of the operations function to the business it is useful to identify five key performance indicators for any operations system. These are quality, speed, dependability, flexibility and cost, where:

1. *Quality* reflects the extent to which operations are performed in line with specifications and/or satisfy the customer (i.e. *getting things right*);

2. *Speed* reflects how quickly and responsively we supply and deliver our products and services (i.e. *doing things quickly*);

3. *Dependability* indicates our reliability to the customer or recipient of the product or service (i.e. *doing things consistently and on time*);

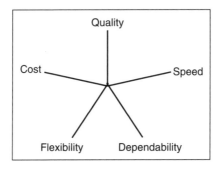

Figure 1.1 Five key performance indicators (KPIs)

4. *Flexibility* reflects our ability to adapt and respond to differing needs (i.e. *being able to change what we do*); and

5. *Cost* reflects the expense we have incurred in a financial sense to deliver the product and/or service to the recipient (i.e. *doing things cheaply*).

In a simplistic sense, and in the 'ideal world', we might argue that an operation should seek to optimize all five of these performance objectives. If an operation delivers the best quality, in the fastest time, more reliably, in the most flexible way and at cheapest cost, it is inevitable that this operation would perform better and therefore more effectively than its competitors. However this is a panacea. As Hill (1993) originally, and others have since argued, operations management comprises a set of 'trade-off' decisions, whereby a decision to improve performance for one indicator often (though not always necessarily) results in a negative effect on another. Most obvious in this respect is cost. Often decisions to reduce cost can impact upon quality, speed, reliability and flexibility if improperly thought through. This book will, later, indicate where costs and other indicators might be simultaneously improved, but we need to recognize there are often *constraints* on what we might be able to achieve. And this indicates the second important factor of operations management: it is about managing constrained resources (human, physical and financial) which places limitations upon what we can achieve.

In the same way as the performance objectives above in Figure 1.1 can be used to compare and contrast different operations systems, so can the 'four Vs'. Let's investigate each of these individually, starting with volume. Figure 1.2 shows low volume on the left-side of the continuum and high volume on the right. Operations systems producing low volumes of products and services invariably result in: low repetition of tasks; operations performing a large proportion of the job (and perhaps the complete set of activities); less systemization; high unit costs. The opposite applies to high volume operations: greater repetition, a greater division of work, greater systemization and lower unit costs through economies of scale. The other three Vs run counter to volume, with 'high' on the left-side and 'low' on the right. This reflects the tendency for low volume operations systems to have high variety, high variation and frequently higher visibility. So high variety operations, those that produce a wide range of products and services, offer flexibility, are able to cope with and match customer needs and tend towards higher unit costs. Low variety operations, producing more standard products and services, have the opposite features. Variation reflects

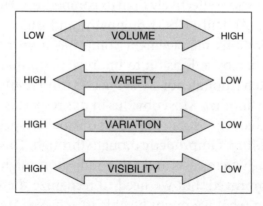

Figure 1.2 Volume, variety, variation and visibility (the four Vs)

ability of the operations systems to flex and change, usually in response to the nature of demand (frequent and rapid changes on the left-side, very stable, unchanging demand on the right. High variation operations systems feature the ability to change capacity of output, anticipation, flexibility response and generally high unit costs. Finally visibility reflects the extent to which operations facilities and workers are physically seen or capable of being monitored by customers and clients, or whether they are out of sight and contact (back office type operations). High visibility operations feature short waiting tolerance, the need for customer contact skills, variety and responsiveness in service, and high unit cost.

It has already been noted that the four Vs are arranged in Figure 1.2 so that volume has low on the left and a high on the right, whilst the others run opposite. This is for a reason. The features of operations systems occupying positions near the left-side of the continuum feature *flexibility* as a major concern: the ability to be flexible, to provide a flexible service. Whilst the right-side concurs with *repeatability*: the ability to economically produce products and services in high volume and at a relatively low unit cost. An example at this point serves to illustrate this.

Example 1

You have decided to take a vacation at an Island Resort. You wish to treat your nearest and dearest to a nice break in paradise; you want to be accommodated in a small house on stilts over the ocean. It's an oasis where people come out to you in little motor boats and cook meals for your family, then slip away to leave you in peace. You don't see anybody else. For this Island Resort volume would be relatively low, given our definitions above. The variety would be high. You expect them to provide a range of facilities. If you want to Jet Ski, they would be able to provide a Jet

Ski. If you want to go Scuba Dive on the coral reef, they would be able to arrange this, plus transportation and any necessary instruction. The cost to you might be high, but the Resort can supply this. Variation is potentially high for the Island Resort because of the unpredictability and needs for varied control systems for the services. Finally, visibility is high. You want to see a chef wearing the necessary outfit and hat preparing and cooking for them on a 'desert' island. You are likely to have a short waiting tolerance: if you are paying considerable amounts of money you want and expect efficient service now. The Island Resort, therefore, needs to design and plan their operations with the needs of its customers in mind. The Resort needs excellently designed and constructed accommodation and administrative buildings; staff with good customer contact skills; there is a need to recruit flexible employees who seem genuinely pleased to meet and greet customers and efficiently respond to their every need. All this comes at a high cost, but the customer is willing to pay for this.

Now contrast the Island Resort with a chain of Express Hotels, serving the needs of people who are on business or touring, and need to stay just one night, usually for about 8 hours. The Express Hotel needs to have a bed, a television, tea and coffee making facilities, and sometimes a telephone, not often though because we all have mobile phones. As a customer you need to be able to check-in and check-out quickly, and know that the room meets a standard quality. You don't care whether you see a member of staff or not. You just want to get into your room for the night, pay your bill and leave. You probably do not even want breakfast because you will take 'breakfast to go' with a coffee when on your way to your next destination. So, in contrast to the Island Resort, volume is high, because the

Hotel and customer alike require fast throughput and high repeatability. They are geared to a high volume of customers with very similar needs, and only willing to pay budget prices. Variety is low. Most of the Express Hotel chain's rooms look and feel identical. Variation is low because you, as the customer, are not expecting any differences. There is a stable routine, predictable operations and high utilization. Most of these hotels are located adjacent to major highway intersections so they are convenient and easy to get to. Visibility is low. Ideally you do not want to see anybody. After a long day's work or journey you are in no mood to talk to anybody and just want to soak in the bath or take a shower, then get a good night's sleep and depart.

To summarize, the four Vs are used within organizations to assess their operations. Organizations can profile customer needs across the four continuums, compare this to their existing facilities (where the operations are currently placed in terms of product or service delivery) and can also develop profiles for direct competitors. Such profiling enables *gap analyses* where, for example, one can identify any problematic differences between customer needs and actual delivery from our operations system, as well as benchmarking against competitors.

The scope of operations management

Operations management relates to that function of an organization concerned with the design, planning and control of resources for the production of goods or provision of services. As a discipline it is not merely confined to a collection of techniques and quantitative methods. It makes appropriate use of the tools of operational research and statistics where relevant, but is primarily concerned with the broader issues involved in the design, planning and control of products, services and processes.

There are a number of ways of conceptualizing the scope of operations management, some of which are suggested below:

By considering the components of an operations system: Utterbeck and Abernathy's (1975) model of innovation suggests that any productive unit should be considered as comprising three main elements: product, process and work organization. It is useful to consider the operations manager as having responsibilities in all three of these areas.

By considering the life cycle for products: The operations management function is concerned with, and should have an input to, all stages in a product's life cycle. The product life cycle of introduction, growth, maturity and decline can be equated to a process life cycle, as illustrated in Figure 1.3. The responsibilities of the operations manager, therefore, should not be merely confined to the *production* stage, but to all stages of the product and process life cycle.

By considering the organizational scope of operations management: 'Operations management' should not be confused with the

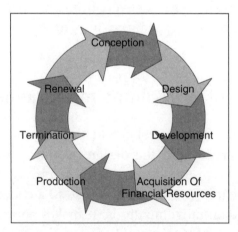

Figure 1.3 The process life cycle

term 'operational management'. The management of operations permeates all levels of organizational decision making and is not merely confined to less important, low level and short term decisions. The operations manager should, in turn, enter more widespread strategic debates in addition to maintaining contact with day-to-day operations. Thus the scope for operations management in decision making covers operational management right through to strategic management (see Figure 1.4).

The conceptual model employed in this book identifies and distinguishes 'design' activities from operations 'planning and control' and 'quality'. Design, covered in Chapters 2, 3 and 4, involves:

- *Business process design*: The organization and arrangement of physical facilities, information and material flows, and labour resources to enable the conversion of inputs (materials, orders, labour, etc.) into outputs (goods and services).

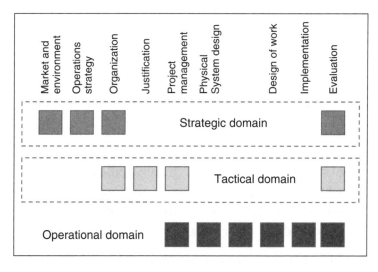

Figure 1.4 The levels of operations management decision making (Bennett and Forrester, 1993)

- *Product and service design*: Interrelated with process design, the configuration of the goods and services our processes are producing and delivering.

- *Technology transfer*: An activity frequently cited and identified as important, but often overlooked in other texts. Design activity will always involve the transfer of 'know-how' from one person, or group of persons, to others in the design process. This is true whether we are talking about new product or processes (research and development transferred from the 'laboratory' into regular operations) or the transfer of existing technologies (e.g. expanding operations, including establishing new facilities overseas based upon home operations, as part of an international operations strategy).

Planning and control is contained within Chapters 5 to 7. Planning and control concerns the organizing and monitoring of operations systems, projects and programmes, together with the feedback of variances from plan for process or programme adjustment where necessary. It includes:

- *Controlling enterprise resources*: The resources of the organization (its facilities, people and materials) need to be effectively managed in terms of operational schedules, workflow, materials management and throughput.

- *Developing lean operations*: The operations need to be managed in such a way that waste (of time, of resources, of money, of effort, etc.) are minimized. Lean operations have evolved in terms of theories and practice over the last two–three decades, so to be competitive organizations must grasp these principles.

- *Managing projects:* Linked with programmes of design and change management, there is a distinctive set of management principles for the coordination and control of projects. This not only relates to the set of tools and techniques available, but most critically to organization, teamwork and management styles needed for effective project completions.

Quality management has been explored in depth and much written about over recent years. The main themes for operations managers include not only quality control, but also an emphasis on improvement. This is the reason why this book punctuates the chapters on design and planning/control from quality management chapters with the coverage of managing operations strategically (Chapter 8). Our argument here is that 'improvement' forms the core of any effective operations strategy, so the main strategy chapter should be placed here to integrate and link preceding principles from the improvement process covered later. The main principles of quality management, covered in Chapters 9 and 10, include:

- *Managing quality systems*: Quality control systems need to be effectively designed and put into practice, to enable the capture and evaluation of quality data and customer feedback, whether this data is quantitative or qualitative in nature.

- *Improving the operations*: Contemporary 'best practice' indicates that operations systems should not stand still, merely adopting quality management systems which measure whether performance conforms to prior specifications. Instead there should be an emphasis on *continuous improvement* whereby there is a commitment by the organization to future development of the operations.

The practice of operations and quality management is accepted as a necessary function within any organization. When one talks of a theory or discipline of operations management, however, it has only been relatively recently that this has become accepted as an appropriate subject for academic study. The reason is perhaps explained by the range of competencies normally required by an effective operations manager: human resource skills, technical knowledge, problem solving abilities, logic, quantitative methods and strategic insight are all areas in which the manager should be conversant. As a result one single line of theory has not emerged within the discipline. The model presented in this book provides a structure for understanding operations in context, but it needs to be appreciated that operations management has developed using theories and principles from a range of other disciplines, as well as being rooted in its own tradition. The final section of Chapter 1, therefore, now conveys an historical understanding of the subject.

The evolution of operations management

Operations management will now be now set within its rich historical context. The major influences and developments in the subject over time will be highlighted. Figure 1.5 shows these historical influences in a chronological order and should be referred to in conjunction with reading the following text. It illustrates the history of operations management and shows the major influences upon the subject through its development.

Operations systems have always been in existence, albeit in different configurations to what one might expect to find today. Consider the ingenuity and industry involved in the following projects from history: Stonehenge on Salisbury Plain in the UK; the Egyptian Pyramids; the Great Wall of China; the cities, aqueducts and roads of the Roman Empire; and the programme of shipbuilding that that preceded the sailing of the Spanish Armada in 1588. These would not have materialized without some form of operations management thinking.

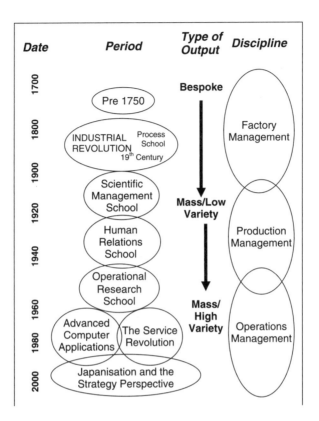

Figure 1.5 The evolution of operations management as a subject and practice

Prior to 1750 products were manufactured quite differently than they are today. Most production took place in the homes, cottages and workshops of independently trading craftsmen, hence the descriptive terms we tend to use nowadays of 'the cottage system' and 'cottage industries'. Production before the advent of the Industrial Revolution can be characterized by direct contact between producers and consumers, little mechanization, and the production of bespoke, custom-made and personalized products.

The Industrial Revolution began in England in the 1700s. The early years can be summarized by two principal developments.

Firstly there was a substitution of machine for human power. The inventors of machine power gave rise to the 'Process School' and their activities gave rise to the various engineering professions. Foremost amongst the early process developers were James Watt with the further development of the steam engine in 1764, Hargreaves and the 'spinning jenny', Cartwright's 'power loom' and Maudsley's 'screw cutting lathe'. These inventions gave the Industrial Revolution its initial impetus. This led to the increasingly widespread establishment of the 'factory system'. Adam Smith's 'The Wealth of Nations' (1776) proclaimed the benefits of the division and specialization of labour. Thus production activities came to be broken into small, specialized tasks assigned to workers through the manufacturing process, as opposed to the craftsman's 'make-complete' approach. Increased capital intensity through mechanization and new ways of planning and controlling production workers using the principles of specialization led to a move away from the cottage system to that of factory working.

Two notable developments occurred in the nineteenth century. First was the concept of *interchangeability*. One of the earliest attempts at production using interchangeable parts was successfully accomplished by Eli Whitney, a manufacturer of rifles for the US government, in 1790. Whitney designed and built on an assembly line such that parts were produced to tight tolerances enabling every part to fit right first time into a rifle assembly. Previously parts were hand crafted, or else they were merely sorted from large batches to find those components that fitted together neatly or only required minor modifications. The concept of interchangeable parts was not easily grasped at first, but is today taken for granted. Consider where we would be without interchangeable light bulbs to holders and interchangeable discs for CD and DVD players.

By 1850 the cottage system was almost completely replaced by factory working. Industrial empires were being constructed by a new class of entrepreneurs and businessmen. By 1900 the high level of capital and production capacity, the expanded urban workforce, new Western markets and increasingly effective transportation and communication set the stage for the great production output explosion of the twentieth century.

Around 1900 the Scientific Management approach was being developed. This was initially based upon the pioneering work of Frederick Winslow Taylor (1856–1915), outlined in his 'Principles of Scientific Management' (Taylor, 1911). At the time, scientific management represented a concerted attack on the prevailing techniques used in the management of production. The work of Taylor, Lilian and Frank Gilbreth and Henry Gantt, amongst others, was analytical and stressed the need for the development of standards for work and improved efficiency. There was little consideration, however, of human feelings and most practitioners of scientific management viewed operators as mere extensions of their machines working within a wider, controlled system.

A number of ideas and techniques were developed at this time including piecework payment systems, time and motion study, the principles of efficiency, standards and management by exception. Criticized as scientific management is today, and in many respects rightly so, its development constituted the first truly rigorous and structured theory of production management to replace the more general and less analytical methods of factory management used before. Scientific management principles culminated with the opening of the Ford Motor Company's Rouge plant in Detroit for the production of the Model-T (see Womack *et al.*, 1991 for an interesting discussion of the rationale behind early Ford systems). The Rouge plant featured standardized product designs using interchangeable parts; mass production;

low manufacturing costs; mechanized assembly lines; and high specialization of labour. Ford was an adapter rather than an inventor of scientific management and the Rouge plant formed the model for factory design and work organization well into the twentieth century (the approach now commonly known as 'Fordism'). So, around the 1920s, was born the era of mass manufacture and standardized, low variety products.

In the 1930s an opposing view to scientific management began to emerge in which behavioural issues were identified as being important to productivity. Knowledge of psychological and sociological features started to influence job design, strategies for worker motivation and management control policies. The organizational forms of production and service companies have been influenced by a number of *'behaviouralist'* theories and practical approaches. A seminal programme of research were the *Hawthorne Studies*. These were a series of experiments conducted by researchers from the Harvard Business School at Western Electric Company which illustrated the importance of human aspects in determining output and productivity (Roethlisberger and Dickson, 1939). These were later followed by further theories of motivation (see, e.g., Maslow, 1943; McGregor, 1960; Likert, 1961; and Herzberg, 1966).

A major contribution to our understanding of operations management was made by the *sociotechnologists*. On the evidence of development of work design in the British coal mining industry, the teamwork approach to flowline assembly at Philips, Eindhoven, and the experiences of Volvo in Sweden with autonomous group working, theorists (most predominantly from the Tavistock Institute) stressed the need for the parallel development of social and technical systems for the success of manufacturing operations (see, for example, Gyllenhammar, 1977). More recently the need for flexible labour to cope with changes in the market and environment has been identified.

Atkinson's (1984) model of the 'Flexible Firm' was developed as an explanation of flexible organization. 'Post-Fordism' has developed whose supporters argue that the era of mass production is now over with more flexible and less rigid work structures now developing (Murray, 1989). The argument for 'Flexible Specialization' has been forwarded which sees a revival of craft-forms of production and the need for multi-skilling in the workforce (Piore and Sabel, 1984).

In terms of tools and techniques for operations management, we are indebted to the Operational Research (OR) School. OR originated in the military and defence organizations of Britain and the USA in the 1940s, during World War Two, to help solve problems of civilian defence, bombing strategies, transportation and military logistics. Subsequently OR theorists turned to business and industry to apply their techniques. The spin-offs for operations management included new quantitative techniques for stock control, scheduling, forecasting, project management, quality control, simulation and linear programming, to name just a few. In the 1950s OR was responsible for the introduction of computers in the management of operations. OR seeks to replace intuitive decision making for large complex problems with approaches that identify 'optimal' or 'best' solutions through analysis. It is in its logical and methodological approach that OR has contributed to the developing theory of operations management. (For more detail on the history and the techniques of OR see Duckworth *et al.*, 1977.)

Computers are now a highly cost effective and efficient means of managing and distributing the information required to plan and operate production and service systems. New computer technologies have also had a profound impact on the design of new processes with the development of flexible and programmable systems. Most significantly, the control afforded by computer technology has made possible the manufacture of products in mass volumes, but in a wide variety and, in some instances, configured to suit individual customer requirements.

There has been a vast expansion in the service and public sector industries since 1960. During this time manufacturers and service operators have come to realize that they have a considerable amount to learn from one another and that there are innumerable areas of similarity in the management of their operations. Note also that all products will have an element of tangible good and service associated with them. Conversely many services also have a tangible product content (e.g. a MacDonald's burger is both a physical 'good', but also is associated with a 'package of service elements'). The need to manage service operations efficiently and effectively is just as necessary as the productive management of manufacturing, especially as many service operations have high visibility for the customer or client. Many principles and concepts are transferable. For example, all service operators will have inventories to manage, quality to control, work to schedule, output to deliver, facilities to layout, employees to remunerate, and so on. However the lessons are not one-way. Manufacturing organizations are learning much in terms of customer care and service reliability and flexibility from the service industries.

The economic expansion of Asia, and most notably Japan, since the 1960s has stimulated the development of alternative operations theory and practice. New concepts such as 'just-in-time' management, new approaches to quality and design management (such as Total Quality and Kaizen) and the encapsulation of these principles into 'lean operations' were evolved, in Japan particularly. This served warning of a new challenge to the traditional Western manufacturers (Hayes and Wheelwright, 1984; Schonberger, 1986; Womack et al., 1990).

Another recent development has been the shift in emphasis from techniques and systems at the operating level to a broader and more balanced strategic perspective of operations. The works of Wickham Skinner (1985) and Terry Hill (1985) in the area of strategic management and its interface with operations are germane here. As indicated earlier in this chapter, operations management is not merely confined to low level, limited impact decision making, but has a strategic consequence. Businesses that expect to remain competitive now need to grasp this, and ensure that product service and delivery live up to the claims made in advertising and promotion campaigns.

Referring back to Figure 1.5, it has been illustrated how the development of operations management has been closely tied with the emergence of a number of schools of thought over the last 200 to 300 years. In the 1800s the prime focus was the management of the factory, but as scientific management practices became more widespread in the early twentieth century the discipline changed from general factory management to production management. The wider operational perspective brought in by OR to encompass transportation, logistics and supply plus the growing need to incorporate and learn from service operations has broadened the discipline further. Now, subject to the influence of computer developments and Japanese approaches, the theory and practice of operations and quality management continues to develop under the influence of a number of different, and often conflicting, schools and paradigms.

Summary

This chapter has introduced the topic of operations management and has outlined the structure and logical presentation of the book. It has defined some core theory: five key performance indicators (KPIs) = quality, speed, dependability, flexibility and cost; four Vs = volume, variety, variation, visibility. It has suggested ways of conceptualizing the scope of operations management by considering: the components of an operations system; the life cycle for products; the organizational scope of operations management. Finally, to better contextualize the topic, it provided a synopsis on the evolution of operations management.

Further reading

- Greasley, A. (2009) *Operations Management*, 2nd edn, John Wiley & Sons, Ltd.

- Johnston, R., and Clark, G. (2008) *Service Operations Management: Improving Service Delivery*, 3rd edn, Pearson Education Ltd.

- Piore, M. and Sabel, C. (1984) *The Second Industrial Divide: Possibilities for Prosperity*, Basic Books, New York.

- Slack, N., Chambers, S. and Johnston, R. (2007) *Operations Management*, 5th edn, Pearson Education Ltd.

- Slack, N. and Lewis, M. (2008) *Operations Strategy*, 2nd edn, Pearson Education Ltd.

- Smith, A. (1776, reprinted 1970) *The Wealth of Nations*, Everyman's Library, London.

- Taylor, F.W. (1911, reprinted 1967) *The Principles of Scientific Management*, Norton, New York,

- Van Looy, B., Gemmel, P. and Van Dierdonck, R.V. (eds) (2003) *Services Management: An Integrated Approach*, 2nd edn, Pearson Education Ltd.

Useful internet sites

- www.euroma-online.org European Operations Management Association (EUROMA).

- www.informs.org Institute for Operations Research.
- www.iomnet.org.uk Institute of Operations Management.
- www.manufacturinginstitute.co.uk The Manufacturing Institute.
- www.mas.berr.gov.uk Manufacturing Advisory Service. Department for Business Enterprise and Regulatory Reform (BERR) – for UK manufacturers.
- www.poms.org Production and Operations Management Society.

Useful academic journal articles

- www.emeraldinsight.com/ijopm.htm International Journal of Operations and Production Management (IJOPM).
- www.poms.org/journal Production and Operations Management (POM).
- www.sciencedirect.com/science/journal/02726963 Journal of Operations Management (JOM).

2 DESIGNING BUSINESS PROCESSES

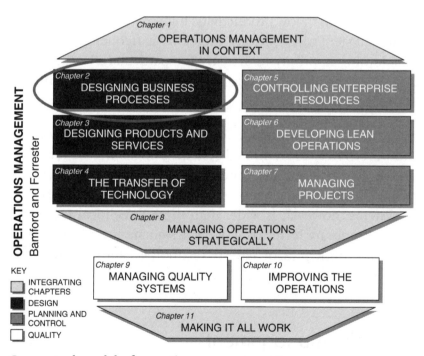

Conceptual model of operations management

Introduction

This chapter discusses the options available for the decision maker when considering the Design of Business Processes (e.g. capacity, location and choice of operations facilities). Large capital investments are frequently involved when designing operations systems and often choices made are not easily reversed. In such circumstances it is important that the decision maker be aware of the consequences of specific process choices and have a thorough understanding of the process of developing new systems. Often a move to increase productivity will result in reduced flexibility and high capital outlay in advanced technology. On the other hand, the desire to develop a truly flexible system, in terms of its response and adaptability to the market or in the range of services/products it can produce, can result in low productivity, high costs and thus strategic disadvantage. Process design, therefore, is frequently a process of adopting appropriate systems for particular circumstances and of balancing the productivity/flexibility dilemma outlined above.

Following the introduction of capacity and a discussion of location choice, conventional systems designs will be reviewed and a classification for general types of operations will be offered distinguishing between 'job, batch and flow'. The choice of systems, however, is wider than these three ideal types and so contemporary forms of systems design are introduced based upon the principles of Group Technology and Autonomous Group Working.

Capacity management

Capacity can be defined as the ability of a process or operation to produce a given volume and is very much determined by the process choices made at the system design stage. Operations need to be planned and controlled within capacity constraints. It is worth noting, however, that some companies plan to hold a relatively large 'capacity cushion' (the ability to serve many more customers of make more product) to enable flexibility in operations. A large capacity cushion may be maintained where operations are subjected to uneven demand rates, uncertain demands, a changing product mix, uncertain capacity losses, or where capacity comes in large portions and cannot be increased or decreased incrementally. These advantages must be balanced, however, against the high capital costs of holding surplus capacity. For example, consider the major supermarkets and the 'extra' checkouts that are available but unstaffed. Why do they have them?

The 'appropriateness' of capacity planning in any part of the operation can be judged by the extent to which the plan:

- minimizes costs;
- maximizes revenues;
- minimizes working capital requirements;
- avoids quality problems;
- increases speed;
- improves dependability;
- enhances flexibility ... etc.

Capacity measures must be expressed in terms that are useful. They have to be accurate and should give indication of relative uncertainty. Seasonality is sometimes an issue and they should take account of weekly/daily demand fluctuation. But is capacity best expressed in the form of: input measures (amount of resource input) or output measures (number of units produced)? Also, for capacity, the concept of 'utilization' is useful

Table 2.1 Some capacity measures

Operation	Input Measure	Output Measure
Artificial Ski Slope	Available hours	Number of customers per hour
Bakery	Oven hours	Number of items baked per week
Restaurant	Number of tables/chairs	Number of customers per week
Plastics factory	Available moulding machine hours	Volume produced per week

as a capacity measure, e.g. 'room occupancy levels' in hotels; 'load factor' for aircraft seats, etc. See Table 2.1 for a variety of capacity measures.

Aggregate planning

Capacity is normally fixed and determined at the process decision stage through the choice of facilities and investment in appropriate technologies. This is part of long term planning. Aggregate planning is, in effect, the medium term planning of operations. It establishes feasible operations plans to meet demand and/or agreed output where capacity is considered relatively fixed. The steps in aggregate planning have been identified by Hill as follows (Hill, 1991):

1. Forecast sales.

2. Make-or-buy decision.

3. Select common measures of aggregate demand.

4. Develop aggregate plans.

5. Select planning horizon.

6. Smooth out capacity.

7. Identify the means to enable short term capacity changes to meet demand fluctuations.

8. Select aggregate plan.

Forecasting is a necessary prerequisite for the management of operations because without some reasonable estimate of future requirements it is impossible to plan. The concept for all types of forecasting is one of looking back at past values (normally demand) and then extrapolating these into forecasts for the future. 'Short term forecasting' is most commonly employed in the management of operations. The two most common short term forecasting techniques used are the 'moving average' and the 'exponentially smoothed average' methods.

Three ways of reconciling capacity and demand

1. *Level capacity* = capacity remains at a predetermined level throughout, regardless of demand. For example, we decide we have capacity to make 12 tables per week. The forecast predicts little demand at the beginning of the year but a peak later on; we therefore plan to store the initial surplus and sell them later in the year when demand exceeds the capacity.

2. *Chase demand* = we alter our capacity to chase the demand. For example supermarkets use this approach with their check-outs staffing; not all checkouts are constantly open, when a peak in demand occurs the store takes people from other areas and put them on the checkouts. It is all about chasing the demand; re-arranging your resources to meet the needs.

3. *Manage/change demand* = using simple pricing mechanisms such as special offers to increase sales or increasing the price to preclude people from purchasing. This controls the demand.

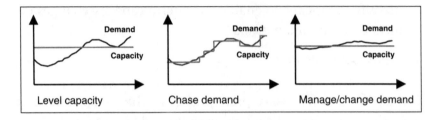

Figure 2.1 Basic capacity plans

The three ways of reconciling capacity and demand (see Figure 2.1) are seldom used in isolation. In reality companies typically use two or more, often at different times of the year. For example, in the UK supermarkets have different manning levels throughout the summer holiday months when compared to the lead-up to Christmas. During the summer holiday period fewer people shop compare to Christmas, when increased customer numbers are matched by increased staffing levels.

Location choices

Choice of location is a senior management decision. It is vital that organizations carefully consider the implications of selecting the correct geographical region/location. Operations personnel can, and often do, participate in this decision process and a number of factors, which might influence the eventual choice, should be thought through.

When choosing a new location it is important to consider where the facility under question lies within the physical distribution (or logistics) chain. The distribution systems of different products and services can vary considerably, but a typical manufacturing and distribution system would comprise a number of levels including raw materials processing, component processing, manufacturing, wholesale and retail. The further back a particular operation is in the logistics chain, the closer to the source of raw materials the location will probably be. Likewise the further downstream the operation, the nearer it tends to be to the customer.

The features of a typical distribution system are as follows:

- Processing separated from warehousing, retailing, etc.: each organization can develop and use its own expertise.

- Economies of scale by concentrating operations away from customers and suppliers.

- Wholesalers keep large stocks from many suppliers, allowing retailers a choice of goods.

- Wholesalers are close to retailers and have a short lead-time.

- Manufacturers need not carry large stocks of finished goods.

- Retailers carry less stock as wholesalers offer reliable delivery times.

- Wholesalers place large orders and reduce unit prices.

Classification and features of operations systems

Service and production operations cover a wide range of different situations. One could say that each operations system has its own distinctive features and so generalization to develop any form of systems design theory is impossible. However there exists a need to develop a rationale for classifying systems so that each case is not treated as separate and unique. Consequently, an approach has been developed which identifies common features as a means of classifying operations systems.

The parameters shaping systems design have been identified as 'human resources' (the organization of work), 'physical facilities' (the layout and arrangement of facilities) and 'demand' (its level and pattern). This, in turn, has enabled the development of generalized approaches in their design, planning and control.

The parameters of human resources, physical facilities and demand have given rise to the widely agreed categorizations of 'job', 'batch' and 'flow' for conventional operations systems. These categories are summarized in Figure 2.2 and put into perspective within Figure 2.3 regards increasing batch size.

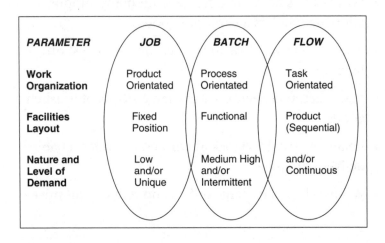

Figure 2.2   Categorization of production systems design

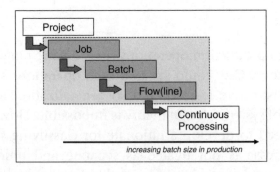

Figure 2.3   Volume and production systems design

Type	Advantages	Deficiencies
JOB	Flexibility (product) Low fixed cost Job enlargement Simple planning	Low resource utilization Long set-up times Duplication High training needs
BATCH	Flexibility (routing) Specialization (tasks & supervision) Isolation of processes Priority changes	High work-in-progress (WIP) Frequent set-ups Extensive movement Long throughput times
FLOW	Few set-ups Low WIP Minimum movement Low skill High specialization Easily automated	Human Problems (recruitment, staff turnover, monotony, absenteeism, etc.) Physical Problems (high capital, cost, inflexibility for product % sequence, reliability, etc.)

Figure 2.4   Features of conventional systems

The characteristics and features of each are described in turn within Figure 2.4.

Job systems

A job system is appropriate were demand is low or unique ('one-offs') and incorporates facilities layout by fixed position, where resources and materials come to a single location and products are then manufactured complete. The work design here is thus 'product orientated', meaning that the job content of people within the system centres upon the manufacture of the product in a make-complete sense.

Job systems demand operators with a wide range of skills and adaptability to cope with the wide range of tasks demanded of them. Thus there is ample scope for job enlargement in work design. Additionally, planning activities are simple, with all materials and resources coming to one point of use and being made complete. However job-type work designs demand a highly skilled workforce, so training needs and costs tend to be high. Where volumes increase, the only way that job systems can cope is through duplication of existing facilities with a subsequent low resource utilization. Thus, despite the attractions for operator work design in job environments, other types of system usually need to be adopted for higher demand situations.

Batch systems

The second category of system is that of batch. A batch system possesses a functional layout whereby similar machines or processes are grouped together and materials move between those processes in the manufacture of individual products. Batch systems are used in medium or intermittent demand situations or where production rates exceed the rates of demand and the main justification for moving from a job to a batch system is the increased utilization of resources at individual facility locations.

The work design within batch systems is 'process orientated', with jobs directly reflecting the functional area within which the operator is working. A major argument for the use of batching is that it offers a high degree of specialization, both in terms of operating tasks and supervision.

Batch systems have a number of deficiencies, however. These include the tendency to hold high work-in-process due to the queuing inherent in the system, frequent set-ups as processes change from one product or service type to another, extensive movement of materials and/or people through the process, and generally long throughput times.

Flow systems

The final type of conventional system in the classification is the flow (or line) system. Flow systems are used for situations where demand is high or continuous and the rate of production matches that of demand. Processes are laid out in sequence and work organization is task orientated, with operators performing a confined task or restricted number of tasks on a repetitive cycle.

Much has been written in criticism of flow systems, but the logic underpinning the system is that the high specialization and balancing of the line enables products to be produced quickly and efficiently with a minimal number of set-ups and materials movement. In terms of work design, the benefits frequently quoted include the ability to use low skilled labour, economies of scale through a high specialization of tasks and, more recently, the ease of automation of the simple and repetitive tasks performed.

Flow systems have been seen to experience many human problems when in operation through monotony and boredom at work. As a result of these specific difficulties in operating flow systems have included 'line-pacing' for workers, recruitment, high staff turnover and absenteeism, poor quality through a lack of commitment, and a high incidence of industrial relations problems developing.

Other types of operations systems

In terms of services process design, professional services, service shops and mass services equate to job, batch and flow. Whilst maintaining the conventional categories of job, batch and flow, some authors now consider it appropriate to add a further two distinctive operation system types, 'project' and 'continuous processing'. The project system is a variation of the job system, but is used to describe those activities where facilities are brought to a location only for the duration of the product's manufacture. Civil engineering and construction projects are obvious examples. Continuous processing systems are a variation on flow/line and involve those facilities where materials are processed through successive stages and flow from one operation to another. The processing of petrochemicals and aluminium smelting serve as examples of continuous processing.

Facilities layout

A number of established techniques exist for the layout of these various systems configurations; we shall concentrate upon the basic concepts. The key consideration in the design of functional layouts (as used in batch manufacture) is the need to reduce total distances incurred in materials movement and optimize production flow. For flow manufacture the important concern is that of line balancing, ensuring that the work content assigned to workstations is roughly equal so that no operator or machine in the flow line is unduly over- or under-loaded. Other considerations come to the fore when designing service and administrative facilities, but generally a 'good' operations layout should comprise the following attributes:

- Throughput time and cost minimized by reducing movement, handling and inefficiencies.
- Supervision and control simplified by better design.
- Enables flexibility.
- Maximizes output.

- Attention to human and organizational issues.
- Quality of product or service maintained.

Basic layout types

There are a number of distinct layout types: fixed position; process; product; cell; and mixed:

- *Fixed position layout* is where the 'transforming' resources are stationary – the equipment, machinery, plant and people who do the processing move as necessary. Usually used when: product too large to move; patients too delicate to move; customers object to being moved. Key points as regards this layout are: adequate space required; all contractors have access to their part of the project; minimal movement of material, machinery and people.

- *Process layout* is where the needs and convenience of the 'transforming' resources dominate layout decision. Usually used when: different products or customers have different needs and take different routes. Key points as regards this layout are: similar processes are located together; products, customers or information flow though the operation taking the route from process to process according to their needs; flow pattern can be complex.

- *Product layout* is where the 'Transforming' resources are located entirely for the convenience of the 'transformed' resources. Usually used because the sequence of activities matches the order in which the processes have been located. Key points as regards this layout are: transformed resources 'flow' along a 'line' of processes; sometimes called a 'line' layout; flow is clear, predictable and easy to control; used for standardized products.

- *Cell layout* is where transformed resources are pre-selected to move to one part of the operation. Usually used because all the transforming resources for their needs are located in one area (a cell). Key points as regards this layout are: the cell itself may be in a process or product layout; after being processed the transformed resources may go to another cell; attempts to bring some order to the complexity of the process layout; a compromise between process and product layout. Reasons for popularity include: desire for faster throughput times; reduction in inventory; increasing product variety; greater emphasis on self-directed teams; improved operator expertise.

- *Mixed layouts* are used by many operations. A hospital is a good example: the operating theatre is a fixed position; each department in the whole hospital represents a particular process; surgery, X-ray, maternity unit, etc., each represent a cell; the blood processing laboratory uses product layout.

The system design process

The process of designing, or of making a process choice, has conventionally been one of choosing between job, batch or flow, or even project and continuous process. This choice was frequently based upon what might be termed 'conventional engineering and manufacturing wisdom', often emanating from the operational level of decision making in the organization. The process was to determine likely volumes, the type of facilities available and the type of work design deemed most appropriate (the three parameters determining the job, batch, flow categorization) and then choose one of these three types.

However, a wider range of factors must be considered in the design and choice of processes. Most notably, the design of operations has been closely linked to the overall needs of the business, thus involving a significant element of strategic choice. Approaches to systems design tend not to merely consider the technical and volume/capacity aspects, but also consider the wider strategic, market, organizational and human issues. Recent research has involved the development of design methodologies and associated models of design to assist in the modern approaches to systems design.

Contemporary forms of process designs

Job, batch and flow can now be viewed as the three conventional process design options and their implications for production organization and work design are generally accepted. Over the last 30 years, however, there have been considerable efforts by theorists and practitioners to develop alternative approaches to fixed position, functional and line forms layout in the organization production and work of employees. The broader, more business orientated approach to process decision making outlined above has resulted in the design of innovative new systems. Two of the most widely publicized systems designs are those of 'Group Technology' and 'Autonomous Working'.

Group technology and cellular manufacturing

The concept of group technology or GT (also referred to as 'cellular manufacturing') was developed as an alternative to functional layouts as used in batch manufacture. Parts and/or products are grouped into 'families' on the basis of similarities in appearance, type or, most commonly, processing requirements. Human and/or machine work centres (cells) are then established for the manufacture of the parts or products using product layouts. In essence the items are produced on small flowlines of machines or operators. GT, then can be seen as a hybrid of batch and flow manufacture: it seeks to achieve the benefits of layout by product (e.g. low WIP, minimal materials movement, reduced setting/changeover times and shorter throughput times) in the batch production of parts or products.

Difficulties have arisen with the use of GT in certain situations in deciding upon the precise arrangement of facilities and the categorization of parts necessary to enable an appropriate segregation of the overall process into cells. As a consequence of this, GT has tended to be most widely used in the component processing industry where large numbers of very similar parts with identifiable families are produced.

A cellular arrangement of processes has a number of important implications for work design within manufacturing. Firstly, the use of cells enables discrete parts of the business to be dedicated to the manufacture of products serving distinctive markets or goods for individual large customers. It has been found therefore that cellular organization can significantly increase the market focus within a business and, importantly, in the people working within the cell who can now identify and relate to their own external customers and markets. The result of this is that the introduction of cellular manufacturing is increasingly driven by a need to be more market focused rather than merely to achieve the performance benefits through the GT engineering approach.

Secondly it has become recognized that GT can achieve numerous advantages by virtue of the fact that it breaks the manufacturing process into a series of small autonomous production units whereby products/parts are made on a 'make-complete' basis instead of being routed around a functional layout. The advantages of such group working are two-fold. It enables greater accountability across product lines within the manufacturing process and in some cases has resulted in 'business managers' taking responsibility for product design, marketing and production for the items produced in one or a restricted number of cells. The other advantage is that cellular production using multi-skilling provides the opportunity for job rotation which frequently results in more varied and interesting jobs for workers. Converse to this, however, has been the counter claim that job satisfaction can fall due to the reduced variety of parts processed in a dedicated cell compared to the general functional department.

Autonomous group working

Autonomous Group Working was developed as a direct attempt to overcome the human and sociological problems associated with flowline production and short cycle tasks where little opportunity exists for job rotation and enlargement. In autonomous working operators work independently of one another or are arranged into a number of small groups which, to achieve high volume production, may be duplicated and identical within the factory.

Like GT, it can be defined as a hybrid system. Whereas GT is a means of batch production with functional layout, autonomous group working is an alternative to flow manufacture which seeks to achieve some of the human benefits frequently linked with jobbing operations. Group working is geared towards the breakdown of long flowlines in favour of 'make-complete' operations. Tasks are performed at independent work stations rather than at a series of positions in a line which are dependent on one another.

In this system of work employees are allowed to self organize their activities. Normally the only constraint is that a certain quota of production volume is expected by the group in a set time period (usually a week). This inevitably leads to opportunities for the rotation of tasks or more radical changes in the way work is performed should the operators desire. Responsibility for planning and local general management devolves from functional specialists and managers to the group level therefore affording a significant degree of job enrichment. Finally payment schemes are normally based upon the basis of group, and not individual, performance.

Autonomous working, however, has been subject to some criticism. Firstly, the productivity of organizations such as Volvo, who have widely adopted group working, is frequently questioned in comparison to the most efficient Western and Japanese producers. Secondly there is an argument that job rotation, enlargement and enrichment can take place in conventional and Japanese influenced manufacturing operations and that group working is not the only way to make the work more fulfilling. Finally it is widely accepted by advocates of group working that this form of working does not function satisfactorily in every labour market and social context.

Differences between service and manufacturing business process design

A number of key differences exist between service and manufacturing business process design: the nature of the product; customer involvement in the 'production'; the importance of the time factor; aspects of quality control and assurance; the issue of inventories (none for services); and the very different distribution channels. A further complication with services is that production and consumption tend to be simultaneous. As the service producing unit or delivery system can be seen as part of the marketing mix the service manager needs to be an operations *and* marketing manager; as service organizations do not tend to have clearly defined functional areas management of services can be highly complex.

In general terms business process can operate at two extremes: *pure* manufacturing (tangible product, with little or no contact with customer, e.g. mining, heavy engineering, etc.) and *pure* service (intangible product, with high level of contact with customer, e.g. medical, legal, dental or professional services). The *service package* of most organizations is somewhere between these two extremes. In order to translate a service operations strategy into operation it is useful to exactly define the 'service concept': the set of expected benefits that a customer buys to meet their needs and requirements; the overall intention of the service as seen from the customer's perspective. This translates into a number of component parts that, together, comprise the 'service package'. The service package comprises two main components: i) the physical items, e.g. food in a restaurant, etc.; ii) the part that involves contact with the customer, e.g. cutting of hair, etc. For example, an airline customer is influenced by: seat comfort; meals in flight; attitude of cabin staff; boarding/disembarking process. If on business, customers may want to work, if on holiday customers want to relax/enjoy in-flight entertainment. So, the airline company needs to provide a complete service package to satisfy the diverse needs of its customers.

Once the service package is designed, it is important to specially define standards of performance when the service is operational. This is because customer perceptions will vary. Usually setting standards for the *service contact* elements is more difficult than for setting standards for performance and quality of physical goods. Often the individuality and intangibility of the service makes it difficult to specify standards.

Process mapping

Process mapping is used in the emergent design and improvement of existing processes. Simply put a map is developed of the existing process (current or 'as is' map), which is then analysed to identify areas for improvement. A new map is then developed with proposed or 'to be' implemented. This technique is also known a 'value stream mapping', i.e. map out the processes, identify those activities that add value and improve these, and eliminate non value adding activities. Within flowcharting a number of flowcharting techniques and conventions can be used.

Process Redesign underpins the practice of Business Process Reengineering (BPR). It reviews all aspects in a single coordinated approach (i.e. people, process, technology and organization) and seeks *performance breakthroughs through* radical and discontinuous improvements, not merely incremental change. BPR adopts a *process* perspective of the business whilst other approaches (it is argued) generally retain a functional or organizational perspective. The overall intention of BPR is to have processes containing only those activities that *add value*. It has been much criticized, primarily as a return to scientific management with little account of the human issues in organization design and the organization viewed as a set of mechanisms (business processes) which can be 'engineered' and primed for maximum efficiency. Furthermore, many people define BPR as *downsizing*, yet another gimmick to exert power, influence and remove labour.

Summary

Summarizing conventional and alternative systems, one can see from the above that production organization and its effect on work design has historically been a topic of immense debate and interest to systems designers and social scientists alike. The relative features of the established forms of batch and flow process designs have been questioned for some time and thus there has been an emergence of variations on these and group working in particular. However, there still persist doubts as to the superiority of these forms of manufacturing in terms of work design over conventional methods.

Service operations have distinctive features: production and consumption is usually simultaneous and it can be difficult to balance demand with capacity. The service concept needs some thought, and the design of both physical and contact components are key concerns in design. Process mapping is a key technique in the analysis of processes – and provides a basis for process improvement.

Example – Capacity Management

'The Royal Automobile Club, the RAC as it is known, is concerned with break down recovery of vehicles and road side assistance. For example, if your car won't start in the morning or you break down on the road then they send out a mechanic. Now the problem is that the RAC has to supply its services and respond, but the difficulty is, how do you deal with the variation? You can't keep lots of services and patrols out there just anticipating very high demand at any one point of time, so what we find is in fact they do two things. First of all they operate a scheme whereby they offer flexibility to their patrols and expect them to be available at certain times of the day at peak times. The second thing is that about 20 % of their business is outsourced. So what actually happens in terms of managing capacity is that at particular peaks, if they can't respond quickly enough, they *will actually communicate with local garages and other breakdown organizations who will send somebody in their place.*

So capacity management, very difficult because demand in many organisations, particularly service organizations, can be very "lumpy". In services as well, of course, you have to respond immediately, you can't produce the "stock" and this presents particular problems in trying to manage capacity. That is to say balancing the supply of your services with the demands that are made on it.'

Example – Layout and Flow

'We are a business in the food industry with about one hundred million pounds turnover. A particular example I want to share is the layout within our new packing area.

When the floor plan was set out, the space was such that we had an ideal line layout which was a horse shoe. This enabled the operator to get to three pieces of equipment by only walking perhaps three metres across. The other production lines, because of space constraints and the footprint of the area, were more of a dog-leg. With the same equipment over a longer area the operators have to walk something like 25 to 30 metres to cover the same pieces of equipment.

So we have got one line which is ideal, which is the horse shoe, and the other line in the same area that was put in at the same time which is less than ideal, but in the real world there are constraints.'

Example – Layout Design

'We are a luxury car manufacturer, part of a much bigger global group. Key for the business was the introduction of a new model, we had to look at layout and consider the various options and choices. 1) was to build a new plant, on site – so that means we have to knock down a lot of the existing buildings; 2) build it somewhere else, off-site – but the land around this area is quite expensive and restricting because around the actual factory there is limited space; and 3) build it in-house.

We looked at the current layout where our current car was being manufactured. Within that line, in that area, we looked at the process flow and how we actually used the order gangways within the site. Another thing that was a benefit for us was a compelling need for our people to have a look at the layouts. They understood the drive behind it and the vast cost saving to the business by keeping the existing building and just reducing the space.

The key thing that we did was getting people to understand about locating a zone, or an area, near point-of-fit and about looking at what space they have got and how to utilize that space. A lot of people thought that the space they had now couldn't be reduced, so by going to another small training course on how to do layouts they actually came up with the space saving themselves and did their own layout.'

Example – Process Design

'This is an example where I consulted to a small wood turning business, it relates to process design. I was asked *by the managing director to go in and have a look at the total business to improve his productivity. He was worried about having the capacity and things like that, so we discussed a number of options and what we eventually decided to do was to actually break down the business. We had an Operations Manager who was looking after the total business and he was keeping it as a clear entity.*

So, we broke it down into raw materials, storage, finished cut storage and manufacturing. We then looked at more detail in the manufacturing area and identified four distinct product groups with a fifth area which was raw material preparation. So we had the raw material being prepared and feeding into the four product groups, that allowed us to take more control in terms of quality and throughput management because it involved doing different material types through the same process, through the same product.

When we had finished this we were feeding the four lines and that resulted in a 15 % improvement in productivity. But it also fed the products through in a more organized manner as well, so the productivity could be seen and the flow could be seen, to actually be able to find products rather than looking all over the factory.'

Example – Job Design

'Let me talk to you about our job design. Earlier this year we looked at our operational structure in terms of our personnel throughout the factory. It had become obvious to us that having installed Team Leaders into the teams in the various areas in the factory we no longer had a need for a departmentally focused manager. We had got a Team Leader layer, Departmental Manager layer and

myself at Manufacturing Manager layer, but the gap was too big between the departmental managers and myself. What we needed to do was to create a level that was higher than Departmental Manager to give a broader business perspective to the management team whilst creating a vacuum in which the Team Leaders and the team could grow up, gain more knowledge and experience and add more value to the business.

What we have seen since we carried out that change is just that has happened. The area managers are taking a much broader business perspective, they are sharing labour across areas, which is something that wasn't happening before. So we are seeing some business benefits and culturally we are seeing individuals starting to come to the fore-front in terms of their abilities and desire to take on more responsibility, and therefore we are benefiting from improvements as a result of that.'

Further reading

- Chase, R.B., Jacobs, F.R. and Aquilano, N.J. (2005) *Operations Management for Competitive Advantage*, 11th edn, McGraw-Hill.

- Gilbreth, F. (1911), *Motion Study*, D. Van Nostrand Co., New York.

- Hayes, R.H. and Wheelwright, S.C. (1984) *Restoring our Competitive Edge*, John Wiley & Sons, Ltd.

- Russell, R.S. and Taylor, B.W. (2008) *Operations Management: Creating Value along the Supply Chain*, 6th edn, John Wiley & Sons, Ltd.

- Slack, N., Chambers, S. and Johnston, R. (2007) *Operations Management*, 5th edn, Pearson Education Ltd.

- Stevenson, W.J. (2006) *Operations Management*, 9th edn, McGraw-Hill.

- Van Looy, B., Gemmel, P. and Van Dierdonck, R. (eds) (2003) *Services Management: An Integrated Approach*, 2nd edn, Pearson Education, Harlow.

Useful internet sites

- www.eee.bham.ac.uk/eiac Ergonomics Information Analysis Centre.

Useful academic journal articles

- Bamford, D. and Griffen, M. (2008) A case study into operational team-working in healthcare, accepted by *International Journal of Operations and Production Management*, 28(3), 215–37.

- Porter, M. (1987) From competitive advantage to corporate strategy, *Harvard Business Review*, May/June, 43–59.

3 DESIGNING PRODUCTS AND SERVICES

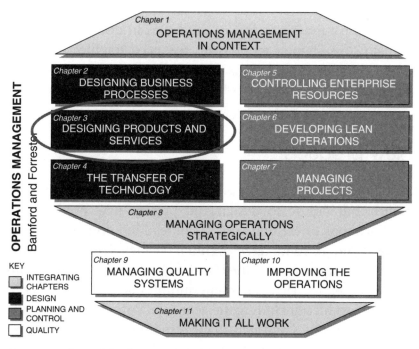

Conceptual model of operations management

Introduction

The design, development and eventual provision of appropriate new services/products, or the timely redesign of existing ones, is the lifeblood of most companies operating in competitive markets. However, an innovative idea or intelligent identification of market need by the design or marketing functions does not, by itself, guarantee success. If the product design or service provision is infeasible, requires excessive investment, or if it is not transferred from concept to provision in an efficient way, then it is doomed to failure from the start, with severe consequences for the whole organization (financial, reputation, etc.). The Operations Manager, therefore, must have timely inputs to the design process to ensure that logical decisions are taken regarding its operationalization.

In addition to raising some of the issues in design and development, this chapter emphasizes the need for the continued evolution of existing designs throughout the product life cycle. Finally the important topic of product liability is discussed.

New products

New product introduction presents considerable risk for companies, but failure to design and present new products, or modifications of existing ranges, can lead to a loss in competitiveness and, in some cases, eventual business failure. The need for new products is explained by the notions of strategic *threats* and *opportunities*. There are many stimuli that prompt the need for new products including the actions of competitors, changes in consumer tastes and step changes in innovation, to mention just three. The success of new products is essential to maintain and increase an organization's income in the future.

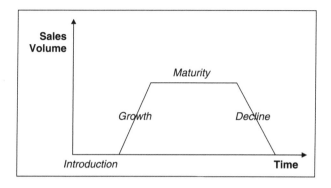

Figure 3.1 A product life cycle

An important concept in product design is the concept of product life cycles. This concept is well known by Marketing Managers, but less well appreciated by operations managers. A product life cycle, an example of which is shown in Figure 3.1, tracks sales volume for a product over time. The life cycle comprises four main phases: introduction, growth, maturity and decline.

The life cycle highlights a number of important issues. Firstly it shows that the life of a product or product version is never infinite. Secondly, information regarding position or progress along the curve is required to trigger the timely development of new products or the revision of existing designs. Finally it illustrates that delayed or late product launches result in a fall-off in income and possible business failure. Companies aim to manage their new product activities and commonly aim to have a balanced portfolio of products with designs at different stages in their life cycles so that those products in maturity can fund the costs of design and growth for others.

Once the need for new products has been recognized a decision must be made regarding the areas for potential opportunity. The product strategy must then be refined in the light of these deliberations and specific new ideas for products must be screened and selected. Finally the design programme for new products must be agreed and initiated whilst simultaneously maintaining a commitment to any existing design projects.

Managing the design process

In the development of new products a number of key organizational issues must be addressed, particularly with respect to the marketing, design and operational interfaces. This causes considerable problems that frequently need to be overcome in the management of product introduction programmes. A dichotomy exists when people from different functional backgrounds are brought together on product development programmes (Oakley, 1984). Burns and Stalker use the definitions of 'mechanistic' organization (to describe the qualities of what is traditionally seen as an efficient operations system) and 'organic' organization (to illustrate the features of innovative design projects) (Burns and Stalker, 1966). The tacit qualities of a 'good' operations manager and a 'good' designer often reflect these features in their work. Operations managers seek order, stability and standardzation, whereas Design and Marketing see the need for change and frequent adaptation to customer needs.

A simple, but typical design process for a new product is shown in Figure 3.2 whereby customer or market needs are determined, then converted into a product specification which leads on to design and development and, eventually, its provision. However, once operationalized, the market must continue to be evaluated, hence the circular iterations of future redesigns and product developments. Within the product design and development process there exists a myriad of feedback iterations and reconsiderations, hence the two-directional arrows on the diagram. So, despite Figure 3.2 being simple in concept,

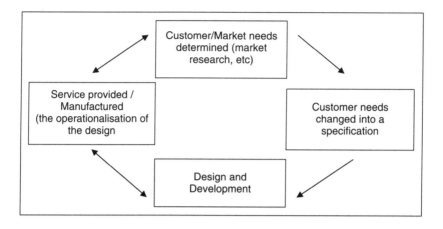

Figure 3.2   The product design process

underpinning it is a great deal of complexity that needs to be effectively managed and controlled.

Quality function deployment

Quality Function Deployment (QFD) is a systematic procedure for translating the *'Voice of the Customer'* into technical requirements and operational terms which uses a 'house of quality' (referring to the shape of the comparison matrix, see Figure 3.3). It focuses on the most important items that need to be improved and provides the mechanism to target selected areas where improvement would enhance competitive advantage. QFD integrates quality assurance into the design process – builds it in.

Important components in the management of product/service design frequently include:

- *Specification* = detailing the exact type of service/product to be designed, the technical expectations, styling, operational needs, cost constraints, etc.

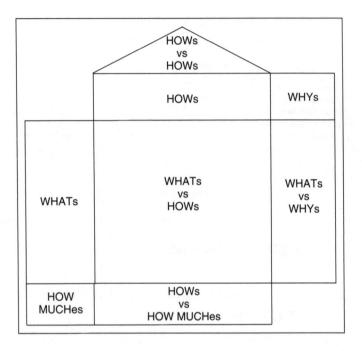

Figure 3.3 Quality function deployment – the 'house of quality'

- *Project Brief* = giving wider terms of reference concerning project costs, timescales, project management reporting, etc.

- *Solution* = evolving a design solution can involve brainstorming, sketches, the use of Computer Aided Design (CAD), canvassing customers on alternative design options: the imaginative part of product design.

- *Development* = the testing, prototyping, experimentation, and continual improvement of emergent designs.

- *Legal Aspects* = Design management requires a detailed consideration of the legal aspects of design including product liability and patent laws.

'Simultaneous' or 'Concurrent' design

A key issue in the product design process is the management of the interface between the design and operations function. All too frequently these work in isolation, with design engineers designing from the marketing department's specification and then passing this on to the operations people who will incorporate into existing systems or develop new processes as appropriate. This approach, 'sequential engineering', can often be very time consuming with a high number of design iterations between the design and production functions. 'Simultaneous engineering' (also known as 'concurrent engineering', however, involves the parallel development of products, processes and production organization. This, it is argued, can not only dramatically cut time to market for new products but may also develop a 'right first time' (quality by design) attitude in the product design process.

Design for operations

It is necessary to distinguish between product design activity for which there are no existing systems and those situations where the new product needs to be capable of being provided within existing processes. In the former situation, the designer has considerable degrees of freedom, whereas designing to suit an existing system can constrain creativity. In the majority of design cases this constraint needs to be acknowledged: here the need to design products compatible with existing systems becomes a key issue. When designing products for operations, consideration needs to be taken of the type of facilities and processes available, handling and storage, existing skills, the policy concerning subcontracting, the fit with the current product mix, current suppliers and existing materials, machine utilization and quality standards, etc.

For maximum operational efficiency, the critical requirements of compatibility must be satisfied. However, a word of warning: compatibility is only one dimension in product decisions. Should design be constrained in all instances using design for operations concepts? What about the important issues of satisfying customer needs and the need to encourage design creativity? Too much compatibility can lead to uncompetitive products and a failure to invest in new process technology. This can inhibit long term development of an organization with a reluctance to follow market trends or to diversify.

Product redesign and value analysis

Design should not stop with the launch of a product/service. It should continue through the life cycle in the form of reviews and redesign. Redesign could be prompted by a change in market needs, or may occur in a structured manner with timed reviews. Product and service redesigns should not be left to evolve in an ad-hoc fashion, occurring only at crisis points. Rather they should be a planned and proactive, not a reactive, activity. Good product design is a major determinant of high quality and economical products and services. A team-based approach, focusing on improving design, therefore seems appropriate which involves participation and involvement from the team members from a range of functional backgrounds. Value analysis (VA) is such an approach. VA is an analytical technique that purports to examine all the cost components of a product or service in relation to all its functional and quality elements.

The objective is to reduce the direct cost of the product/service whilst maintaining or improving its value to the customer. The essence of VA is that it uses a multi-disciplinary team whose members come from different functions and specialisms within the organization. VA operates by identifying value features or specific functions of the product (economic, technical, aesthetic, ergonomic and environmental), examining alternative ways of achieving these, and choosing the way that entails least cost coupled with maximum satisfaction for the customer. The VA team tackles the project by progressing thorough five stages of product redesign analysis: familiarization, speculation, evaluation, recommendation and implementation.

Familiarization

All team members should become fully familiar with the product/service under analysis and its components and so need to consult drawings, specifications, cost breakdowns and see the physical parts and their construction. The team can draw on the expertise of its individual members whereby the accountant might collate and explain the significant of the cost information, the designer can illuminate upon the original design concept, the operations people can detail the steps in the process, the marketing representative can give informed opinions upon customer perceptions and the value features of the product, and so on. All the information gathered should be recorded for use in the next four stages of the VA exercise.

Speculation

This is the most creative stage of the VA process, but should nevertheless be conducted in a structured way. The VA team takes each component of the product/service in turn and subjects it to critical examination. A checklist should be used to include such questions such as *'Can we eliminate it?'*, *'Can we use alternative materials?'*, *'Can we use an alternative supplier?'* and *'Can we manufacture it/provide the service in a different way?'*. Brainstorming techniques may well be employed to generate a wide range of uninhibited suggestions for each component, although the team should follow up any seemingly productive ideas to analyse their effect on the rest of the product/service and its overall cost and value. A smaller number of feasible or desirable changes will result from this.

Evaluation

At this stage the team evaluates the design changes emerging from the Speculation stage in more detail. The total effect of each alteration should be examined. When, and only when an alteration adds value for no additional cost, or maintains value at lower cost, will that change be forwarded for recommendation.

Recommendation

Normally the team will produce a report containing their recommendations and then formally present these to senior decision makers within the organization. This allows for discussion and clarification of the recommended changes and those areas in which the existing product or service design could be improved. Decisions need to taken which, in the opinion of the senior managers, will maximize design improvement, maximize cost savings or, more likely, a balance of each.

Implementation

The team should be in some way involved in following through and implementing those changes that have been sanctioned and then finish their analysis by calculating the degree to which the anticipated cost savings and increased value to the customer have been realized in practice.

VA is a technique applied to the improvement of *existing* products and services. However, once its concepts have been used and appreciated by team members, these can be extended to the design of *new* products and services. Value Engineering (VE) is the term used for the application of value analysis techniques to the design stages of new products/services. The ultimate purpose of VE is to secure improved performances for new products and services at the minimal cost. By virtue of its approach, it also seeks to develop a 'right-first-time' approach in the design of products and services.

Product liability

It is critical that a new product design should abide by and conform to modern product liability laws. Therefore, design work must recognize the constraints imposed by this legislation in all the markets in which the good is to be sold. When one considers the potentially ruinous costs of prosecutions for liability, one can appreciate the critical need to consider these aspects.

Summary

Product design is a key concern for the operations manager. Though often seen primarily as the responsibility of the marketing and design functions, the reality is that for any organization successful design is only achieved if concepts are translated and operationalized effectively into daily operational processes. This section has reviewed product design from an Operations Management perspective. Management of the design processes, and the need to pay attention to organizational issues throughout, has been highlighted and issues of concern should as the need for product specifications and design project briefs were raised. An important consideration in any design project is the analysis of value and so the elements of value, and value management practices were reviewed.

Example – Product and Service Design

'We are a large American semi-conductor manufacturer with a turnover of nine hundred million dollars and five and a half thousand employees.

In the semi-conductor industry constant year on year price reductions are demanded by customers as some of this market is a large commodity market, therefore price is the dominant factor. As a result, to maintain profit margins constant cost reduction exercises are performed at each supplier, this can be using new material or design tweaks or new methodologies to reduce the cost of the component to maintain the profit margin. The supplier sells products with its own name and part number on the product, and also sells the same kind of products with generic part marking for the commodity market. In one instance there was a change between generation number two and generation three for a particular product. A recent problem with customers on another change of process had meant that the quality department was very sensitive to customer notification and the need to give them time to change and consider the new part.

Now, if there is a large customer, for example an automotive customer, or there are some contractual obligations, then any part changes must have full notification: time of change and also the chance for last time buy if the customer is not able to switch to the new part. However, for the 'commodity products', these are commodities – shipped in bulk with no control over who buys them or for what application. There are usually four or five different manufacturers supplying the same product, with each supplier having a slightly different manufacturing technique. So although the commodity part *meets the standard specification, they can have a slight variation, manufacturer to manufacturer.*

So, our quality department requested that all of the new parts had the part number and then G3 at the end for generation number three. However, this caused problems at the customer in terms of the bill of material, which is written using the standard part number. For the commodity products, for the brokers, distributors and the customers, they simply want to order the commodity part name. If they need to order commodity part 'G3' that is an extra problem for them in a purely cost driven market. So they will simply go back to another supplier's product.

In our case we had the quality department who wanted to be ultra conservative and tell every customer about the change and the sales department who would like to maintain the commodity status, to sell as many as possible as quickly as possible.'

Example – Product Design and Design for Manufacture

'Major automotive manufacturer. We lead the design stage of the car components to ensure we could achieve it in the design state as a one-off. We need to bear in mind that we need to be able to produce the same quality at the same standard on a repeatable basis.

So when we actually design a component the key thing is to make sure that the communication flow, down from the shop floor and the input from the actual process engineers to the design engineers is strong. So in that way we get a better design and in turn we get high quality products and more right first time designs.'

Example – Process Redesign

'We are a large US based semi-conductor manufacturer. The power semi-conductor division has a turnover of three hundred and fifty million dollars and fifteen hundred employees. We sell products to the automotive market and a particular one to a German automotive maker.

Initially the customer returned a product which was defective, or they considered to be defective. The product was returned as part of a large circuit board, which contained a large metal clip holding the product to a heat exchanger. The first analysis of the device showed very thin cracking at the top surface of the product and initially it was put down to a very heavy clip which was above the normal pressure recommended by the supplier.

Two weeks later, further devices were returned, this time in different applications which did not involve the clip. The analysis of those devices indicated that part of the process had 'drifted' causing an out of specification error. The result of that was that we needed to redesign the product so as not to be susceptible to a drift in the process and put a process check in place so that it would not drift. In addition, the customer re-designed the process to use a less strong clip so that the problem was solved in three different ways.'

Further reading

- Maslow, A H. (1943) 'A Theory of Human Motivation', *Psychological Review*, Vol. **50**.

Useful internet sites

- www.autocad.com AutoCAD, software for designing new products.

- www.designcouncil.org.uk UK Design Council.

- www.roundtable.com Resources for product and technology development.

Useful academic journal articles

- Kuei, C. (2002) House of quality (QFD) in a minute, *International Journal of Quality & Reliability Management*, 19(4).

- De Feo, J.A. (2002) Surviving the present and the future, *Measuring Business Excellence*, 6(3).

- Carmen, C. and Jose, G.M. (2008) The role of technological and organizational innovation in the relation between market orientation and performance in cultural organizations, *European Journal of Innovation Management*, 11(3).

4 THE TRANSFER
OF TECHNOLOGY

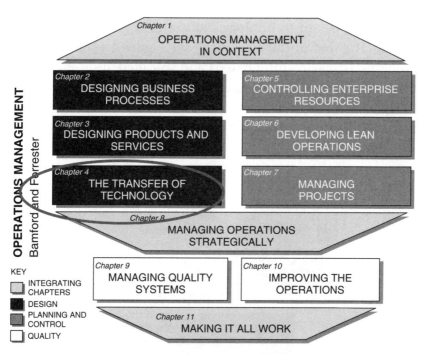

Conceptual model of operations management

Introduction

The decision to invest in new facilities, a new product or a different part of the world will, almost inevitably, involve the process of technology transfer. Companies and governments are the main (but not the only) agents in the transfer of technology. Technology transfer can be defined as the transfer of knowledge relating to the design of a product, its manufacture, the provision of a service, or expertise of the support services pertaining to the product/service. It therefore relates not only to the introduction of new hardware, but also the techniques and skills to operate it.

Vertical and horizontal transfer

Two core types of technology transfer exist: vertical and horizontal. The first of these (vertical, see Figure 4.1) is typical of domestic (single country based) and so-called 'in-house' transfer of new technology. In international operations this is more likely to occur between countries of the same level of development. Horizontal, see Figure 4.1, transfers existing technology

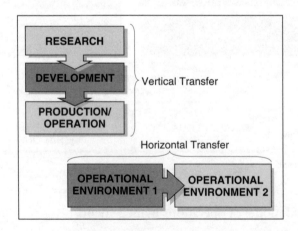

Figure 4.1 Vertical and horizontal transfer of technology

from one context to another. In international operations this is a common means of transferring technology from industrialized to developing countries.

Most transfers are hybrids of vertical and horizontal transfer. Technologies invariably need to be adapted and/or refined and there will need to be a linkage between vertical and horizontal technology transfer. But should one always adapt/select technology to suit local needs or use a standardized/established technology?

The components of technology transfer

The first of these is 'Hardware': the physical product or process technology most people conceive when thinking about technology (e.g. buildings, assembly lines, equipment, tools, components, raw materials). People and knowledge (Humanware) reflect the fact that successful technology transfer is very much a human process of interchanging ideas and learning from this. To be successful (to achieve the set objectives in the transfer project) product, operations, equipment 'know-how', and training all need to be carefully considered. Finally 'software', but not merely software in the computer sense; it must include manuals, procedures, documentation, information, etc.

Technology transfer contexts

Of course, technology transfer involves many more scenarios, principally the transfer of technology: between industries; between functions; along the value chain; between suppliers and acquirers (senders and receivers) in different countries; and international technology transfer. This foreign technology supply can be represented as per Figure 4.2. The left hand

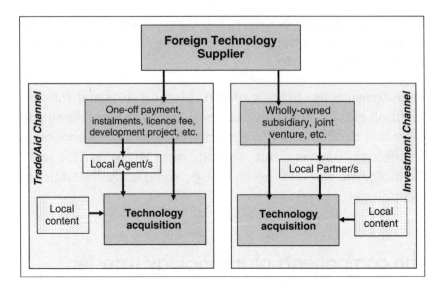

Figure 4.2   International technology transfer channels

side of the diagram represents the acquisition of technology through a one off payment (licence fee, etc.) and perhaps the use of local agents to contextualize the transfer. This is typically for a short term tactical commercial gain. The right hand side shows a degree of vertical integration, with the purchase of a subsidiary (buying the company that makes/provides the required technology). This is commonly a strategic business decision for the long term.

Theories of technology transfer

Traditional theory

When firms determine an appropriate mix of labour and capital they will transfer technology to lower or minimize their costs. But there are some assumptions with this: perfect competition; homogenous products; a high number of firms;

economic rationality. Contemporary theories attempt to overcome these limitations.

Contemporary theory

A high proportion of companies compete not only on price, but also through differentiation. Traditional theories are deficient in addressing this reality. Technology transfer, first and foremost, involves the transfer of expertise and knowledge, not just equipment or product technology. Well-codified technological knowledge is easier/less costly to transfer than new/unproven/disordered knowledge. Even well ordered technologies will require face-to-face contact and transfer of people from the sending to the recipient partner. Given the above, firms should attempt to transfer only those technologies which are well understood, or else pay a high price for the transfer.

Dimensions of technology transfer

Technology transfer is rather an imprecise term which has a number of different contexts. For our purposes we identify four dimensions of technology transfer:

1. *International versus domestic TT*: Transfers need not be only thought of as 'international' and national-boundary spanning. It goes on all the time between companies in national economies (research institutes to commercial organizations) as well as at the micro-level (from Research & Development/laboratory to operations).

2. *Commercial versus non-commercial*: Commercial transfer of product/process know-how, but also considerable

non-commercial TT especially in relation to health, humanity, food and welfare (World Health Organization; UK Overseas Development Administration; numerous non governmental organizations; charities; etc.).

3. *Tangible goods versus intangible know-how*: TT is most usually thought of as the purchase and/or installation of physical equipment. Of course it can involve the transfer of knowledge, management tools and techniques, the so-called 'know-how'.

4. *Free versus proprietary knowledge*: Free in the public domain (e.g. journals, scientific knowledge) versus more applied technological knowledge which is within the domain of commercial organizations, may be protected by patents, or may be trade secrets – whose diffusion often has strings attached in monetary and contractual terms.

Elements in the transfer process

There are a number of important elements to consider within the transfer process:

- *Transfer item*: what exactly is being transferred – product, process, know-how, or combination?

- *Who is the donor*: where is the technology coming from? Who has the proprietary rights, and is that person or organization willing to grant access to the technology?

- *Who is receiving the technology?*

- *How will the technology be transferred*: licensing, direct purchase, or how – there are many different ways, and combinations of these ways, to effect the transfer. This goes some way to explaining why TT is difficult to define.

The (many) mechanisms of technology transfer

These include: turnkey (build-operate-transfer) projects; technological enclaves; licensing; joint ventures; patents; in-house transfers to foreign subsidiaries; emulation of a product or process; the purchase of naked and embodied technology; purchase of technological services; education abroad; site visits and job training abroad; international collaboration in research; published literature; meetings, seminars and conferences. Figure 4.3 illustrates the increasing levels of commitment, potential return and financial risk involved within the various formal agreements available for technology transfer. Amongst these, selling a 'licence' for the use of technology in exchange for royalty payments is more common in later stages of PLC and there are issues of control. Wholly owned subsidiaries are used as a means of transferring technology to gain or maintain access in foreign markets and retain proprietary knowledge; whilst joint ventures reduce the capital cost and investment risk of the transfer process and can often enable the firm to acquire a wider range of technology.

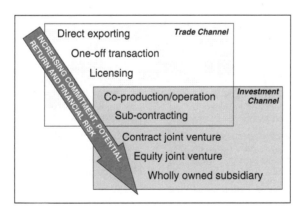

Figure 4.3   Formal agreements for technology transfer

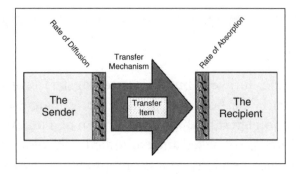

Figure 4.4 The technology transfer process

In terms of at what rate the technology can be transferred, there are many different factors. These can be identified as being production, technology, and/or imitation effected, but demand from the market also influences this as well. Of course the absorptive ability of the recipient is also a critical factor; can the technology be absorbed easily and quickly, or are the scientific and technological (including Human Resources) and social infrastructures not in place. See Figure 4.4.

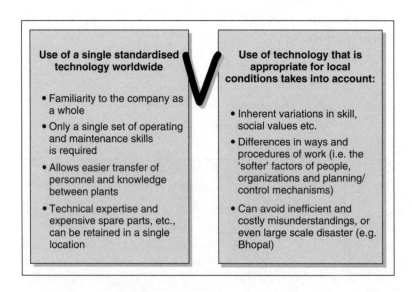

Figure 4.5 Technology choice

Important Considerations also include: Technology span, the proposed number of users per technology application; technology scope, the spread of user application; few actual users, with the process characterized by 'point-to-point' technology transfer; many users, in which case the 'diffusion' of technology becomes a critical issue; and should one always adapt/select technology to suit local needs or use a standardized/established technology? See Figure 4.5.

Summary

Technology Transfer is a strategic issue often omitted from the academic and practitioner literature. It has long term strategic consequences for both the sending and recipient parties, economic as well as social and political implications. Technology transfer equals CHANGE, and change is frequently difficult to implement in practice. E.g. review the national and international press for the high profile examples of technology transfer successes and failures.

Example – Technology Transfer

'We are a food industry business and the example I want to give you is about an opportunity which has been left begging. We have a production line in the factory where we have a station filled position where a lady sits all day just packing drums into a tray and then pushing it into a flow wrapper. This lady is paid £17000 a year to do her job and it's not particularly inspiring for her in terms of mental stimulation. On the other hand, somewhere else in the factory we have a redundant mechanical tray packer which is standing idle and with a slight modification could do this job and release the person. The cost to move that

piece of equipment is £10 000. Now the idea was generated probably three years ago, but because we have had bigger fish to fry we have not taken up that opportunity. So in essence we have lost £41 000 worth of savings. The learn here is to take the technology opportunities.'

Further reading

- Burns, T. and Stalker, G.M. (1966) *The Management of Innovation*, Tavistock Publications, London.

- Fitzsimmons, J.A. and Fitzsimmons, M.J. (2008) *Service Management: Operations, Strategy and Information Technology*, 6th edn, McGraw-Hill.

- Hayes, R., Pisano, G., Upton, D. and Wheelwright, S. (2005) *Pursuing the Competitive. Edge: Operations, Strategy, and Technology*, John Wiley & Sons, Ltd.

Useful internet sites

- www.autodesk.co.uk AutoDesk Inc. AutoCAD software for product design.

- www.graphisoft.com Graphisoft Inc. ArchiCAD software for product design.

Useful academic journal articles

- Cannon, A.R., Reyes, P.M., Frazier, G.V. and Prater, E.L. (2008) RFID in the contemporary supply chain; multiple perspectives on its benefits and risks, *International Journal of Operations and Production Management*, 28(5), 433–54.

- Warren, M.P., Forrester, P.L., Hassard, J.S. and Cotton, J.W. (2000) Technological Innovation Antecedents in the UK Ceramics Industry, *International Journal of Production Economics*, **65**(1), 85–98.

5 CONTROLLING ENTERPRISE RESOURCES

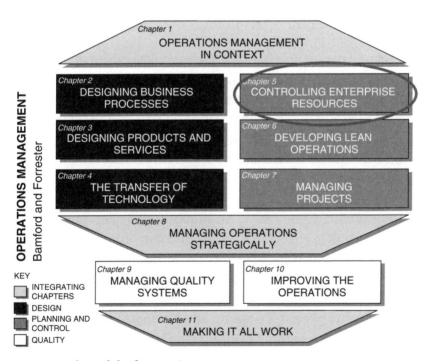

Conceptual model of operations management

Introduction

Once an operations system has been designed and installed, attention will then turn to its operational planning, monitoring and control on a day to day basis. This chapter introduces the basic concepts of planning and control. Following a description of basic control theory, the management of capacity is covered in some detail as a link between longer term design decisions and the operational planning of the system. This leads on to the process of 'aggregate' (or medium term) planning, for which the forecasting of demand is an important prerequisite. At the operational level, operations planning will almost certainly involve scheduling and we shall consider some of the useful techniques developed. The introduction to planning and control ends with a review of the contemporary method of planning, Optimized Production Technology (OPT).

The second part of the chapter focuses on the control of materials and inventories. The 'art' of ensuring that just enough stock is on hand at any point to satisfy requirements, but that these holdings are not excessive, tying up large amounts of working capital. This next section therefore deals with 'classical' inventory control and 'economic order/batch quantity' theory. This theory is, in effect, an attempt to balance out the costs of holding inventory with the costs and consequences of running out of stock (i.e. maintaining adequate service levels). In recent years Economic Batch Quantity (EBQ) theory has received many criticisms, particularly regarding its claim that it is an optimizing technique. The use of policies based upon EBQ have also been demonstrated as having shortcomings in practice, particularly in the face of 'requirements planning systems' and Japanese inspired 'JIT' and 'Lean' systems. A critique of statistical inventory control and its problems in use are therefore reviewed. Materials Requirements Planning (MRP), the central module of most commercially available production control software packages, will be introduced.

Section 1 – operations planning and control

Control theory

The operation of any manufacturing system can be represented by a simple input-output ('I-O') model (as shown in Figure 5.1), where inputs can be viewed as resources (labour, materials, capital equipment, etc.) and output is the results.

At a more conceptual level, the objectives of the business can also be taken as inputs, with measurements and results from the transformation process the outputs. However, as can be seen in Figure 5.1, this system is completely open with no feedback of results from the operations systems to compare against inputs and objectives: there exists no mechanism for control. A 'closed-loop' system is required for effective control of operations so that outputs can be compared to inputs and the differences monitored. This can then be used as the basis for corrective action. A closed-loop system is illustrated in Figure 5.2.

This basic I-O model from systems theory represents any control system, whether manufacturing a product or providing a service. The diagram illustrates the process by which outputs and results are compared to resource inputs, objectives, plans and targets. The types of control systems represented by this model include:

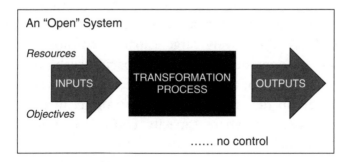

Figure 5.1   An 'open' system – no control

81

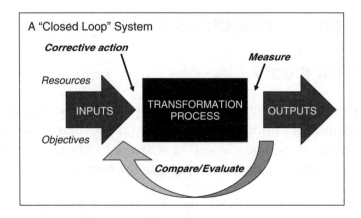

Figure 5.2 A 'closed-loop' system – in control

stock control; quality control; order progressing/chasing against schedules; cost control (budgeting); management of people and labour productivity; and computerized controls.

Capacity management

Capacity can be defined as the ability of a process or operation to produce a given volume and is very much determined by the process choices made at the system design stage (see Chapters 2 and 3). Operations need to be planned and controlled within the capacity constraints. It is worth noting, however, that contrary to 'traditional' management practice, some companies plan to hold a relatively large capacity cushion to enable flexibility in operations. A large capacity cushion may be maintained where operations are subjected to uneven demand rates, uncertain demands, a changing product mix, uncertain capacity losses, or where capacity comes in large portions and cannot be increased or decreased incrementally. These advantages must be balanced, however, against the high capital costs of holding surplus capacity.

Aggregate planning

Capacity is normally fixed and determined at the process decision stage through the choice of buildings and high investment machinery and equipment. This might be seen as part of long term planning. Aggregate planning is, in effect, the medium term planning of operations. It establishes feasible operations plans to meet demand and/or agreed output where capacity is considered relatively fixed. The steps in aggregate planning have been identified by Hill as follows (Hill, 1991):

1. Forecast sales.

2. Make-or-buy decision.

3. Select common measures of aggregate demand.

4. Develop aggregate plans.

5. Select planning horizon.

6. Smooth out capacity.

7. Identify the means to enable short term capacity changes to meet demand fluctuations.

8. Select aggregate plan.

Forecasting demand

Forecasting is a necessary prerequisite for the management of operations because without some reasonable estimate of future product requirements it is impossible to plan for the future. The concept for all types of forecasting is one of looking back at past values (normally demand) and then extrapolating these into forecasts for the future. 'Short term forecasting' is most commonly employed in the management of operations. The two most common short term forecasting techniques used are the 'moving average' and the 'exponentially smoothed average' methods.

Scheduling

A schedule is the plan for performing a series of tasks set against a given timeframe. It is often known as the 'production plan' and is usually developed within an administration office in close liaison with the sales and marketing functions. It is useful to define two terms relevant to the scheduling task. Firstly 'loading' must be distinguished from scheduling. A production load is the immediate timetable of work for a process and is usually regarded as having a shorter timescale (minutes and hours) than a schedule (days and weeks), hence the term 'machine loading'. Secondly, the term sequence, meaning the order in which tasks or orders are to be performed, is often used within scheduling. Usually the scheduling task is one of deciding the sequence of tasks based upon some form of order/job prioritization within the constraint of capacity.

Although it is relatively easy to recognize the scheduling task, it is sometimes not appreciated how complex an activity this can be. Scheduling problems are, in practice, extremely difficult to solve, as can be seen from the following example:

Consider 3 orders (A, B and C) to be scheduled taking the same route through the process. The possible permutations are:

ABC, ACB, BAC, BCA, CAB, and CBA = 6 sequences

(i.e. $3! = 3 \times 2 \times 1 = 6$)

For 20 orders passing through the same sequence as one another, however, the number of alternatives are:

$20! = 2,432,902,000,000,000,000$ or $2,432,902$ billion!

The situation is further complicated when one considers the following which tend to occur in the dynamic operations situation:

- Facilities are rarely all vacant ready to be used when the schedule is developed.
- Sequences are rarely the same for all orders or products, and a single sequence does not always need to be adhered to.
- Estimated process and machine times vary considerably in practice.
- Machines or facilities do sometimes break down.

Furthermore, schedules need to bear in mind and make contingencies for the following:

- delivery due dates;
- variations in capacities between departments;
- variations in process efficiencies;
- planned maintenance;
- planned holidays;
- the possibility of absenteeism;
- existing commitments;
- material availabilities; and
- the levels of scrap, rework and reprocessing.

Under such circumstances it is not sensible to seek optimum solutions to scheduling problems: they could never expect to always find the 'best answer'. Instead production planners will use a series of rules and logic to decide upon as reasonable a solution as possible. The usual process is to ascertain exactly which criteria the schedule should seek to achieve. Frequently, in practice, the schedule will be developed using simple priority sequencing rules, the most common of which include:

- First come, first served;

- Shortest processing time first (SPT);

- Earliest due date first; and

- Static slack (Time to due date minus processing time).

Priority rules or downright logic tend to be used in general cases. However there are some specific manufacturing cases where a number of heuristic algorithms can be utilized for developing schedules. The most well known is Johnson's Algorithm for minimizing total processing time when loading any number of jobs on to two machines, the method for which is shown below. Other scheduling algorithms include Johnson's Algorithm for n jobs on three machines, so called 'branch and bound' techniques (including 'dynamic programming'), and the 'line of balance' method.

Method for Johnson's Algorithm

1. Find the shortest processing time on operation 1 or 2.

2. If shortest time on 1, place that job first; if on 2, place last.

3. Apply steps 1 and 2 to remaining jobs.

4. In the event of a tie priority goes to the job with the shortest time on the other non-tied operation.

Other methods have been devised for scheduling. Materials requirements planning (MRP), has as a main objective the development of the 'Master Production Schedule' (MPS). Just-in-time techniques may also have a bearing on immediate process loading. Another development in production planning and control is that of 'optimized production technology' (OPT).

Optimized production technology (OPT)

Based upon the ideas of Eli Goldratt (see Goldratt and Cox, 1984), OPT is an approach to production scheduling which can be neatly described as the 'management of bottlenecks'. The basic premise underpinning OPT is that it is pointless concentrating on increasing throughput at all processes within the total operation, because the output rate of the system as a whole is determined by the rate of production at the one or two bottlenecks in the system.

The idea behind OPT is that scheduling activity and process improvement activities should concentrate upon 100 % loading at these bottlenecks, then trying to increase output at them through continual improvement. The rest of the system, the 'non-critical activities', need only be loaded to support the rate of production at these bottlenecks (the 'critical' activities). Obviously, improvement of throughput rates on the critical activities may cause the bottlenecks to shift to other activities in the system, changing these to critical and increasing the output of the process as a whole.

Section 2 – inventory and materials management

Purchasing and inventory management

Purchasing and inventory management is the (science-based) art of ensuring that just enough stock is held to economically meet both external and internal demand commitments. This section will introduce the 'Push' Systems, usually classified as Statistical Stock Control. These include two specific policies, Reorder Level (ROL) and Reorder Cycle (ROC), and Materials Requirements

Planning (MRP). The next chapter will cover Japanese inspired 'Pull' systems, including just-in-time (JIT) and lean.

Pareto Analysis, the classification of stock items using ABC categorization, is used extensively within purchasing and inventory management:

- 'A' class items: top 20 % = 80 % total value;
- 'B' class items: next 15 % = 15 % value;
- 'C' class items: final 65 % = 5 % value.

This identifies the important few and the trivial many for the organization.

Stock control parameters

The design of any stock control system is shaped by a number of parameters which result in a balancing of (often conflicting) requirements. These parameters are described below.

Demand (A)

The design of any stock control or purchasing system needs to take into account the following aspects of demand:

- the average demand per time period, usually expressed per annum (A);
- the variability of demand per period, usually expressed as a standard deviation (σ);
- the 'lead-time', order to receipt, of material (L).

Ordering costs (Co)

There are fixed costs involved each time a separate order is raised. If orders are placed too frequently these costs become excessive.

Storage costs (iCm)

The costs of holding material in stock including direct costs of storage, deterioration, obsolescence, insurance and opportunity costs. Expressed as a percentage (i) of the prime cost or price paid for materials (Cm).

Service levels

The efficiency of any stock control system is indicated by the level of service it provides for its customers (internal and external) in satisfying demand ex-stock. In designing a stock system, the company usually chooses the service levels it feels are appropriate to satisfy the customer, but do not result in excessive costs of holding. The most common service levels adopted in practice are 95 % and 99 % (i.e. a 5 % and 1 % risk of stock, respectively).

These parameters, and the mathematical notions given (in brackets), are used in the design of statistical inventory control systems. Economic Order Quantity (EOQ) theory is used to provide a cost effective amount to purchase. See Figure 5.3.

The formula for calculating the Economic Order Quantity:

$$\text{EOQ} = \sqrt{\frac{2\,A\,\text{Co}}{i\,\text{Cm}}}$$

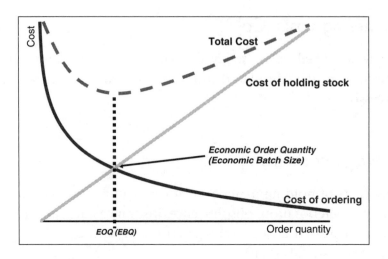

Figure 5.3   Economic order quantity (EOQ)

There are two basic inventory control policies commonly used, 'reorder level' (ROL) and 'reorder cycle' (ROC).

Reorder level policy

The reorder level policy involves placing a fixed order, the EBQ, to replenish inventory when the stock level for a certain item falls below a fixed value, the 'reorder level' (M). It requires the calculation of two values, the order quantity (EBQ) and the reorder level (M). Figure 5.4 illustrates the operation of a reorder level policy stock system. The formulae for these are as follows:

$$EBQ = \sqrt{\frac{2A\,Co}{i\,Cm}} \text{ and } M = AL + k\sigma\sqrt{L}$$

Where: A = average demand per period

L = lead-time in time periods

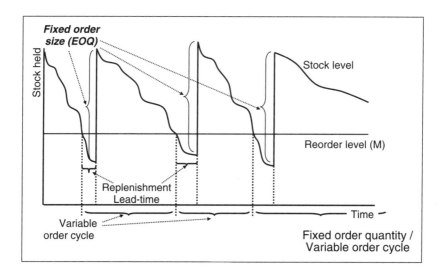

Figure 5.4 Stock control using a reorder level policy

k = no. of std. normal deviates (NB: k = 1, Vendor Service Level = 84.1 %; k = 2, VSL = 97.7 %; k = 3, VSL + 99.9 %)

So the reorder level policy incorporates a fixed order quantity (EBQ) and a variable order cycle (time between orders), as triggered by depletion below M.

Reorder cycle policy

Under this type of system an order is placed at predetermined times with a fixed period between orders. At each periodic review the stock held is compared to a calculated 'maximum stock level' (S) and the difference between the two becomes the order size. So, contrary to the reorder level policy, reorder cycle has a variable order quantity and a fixed order cycle.

The reorder cycle system requires calculation of the review period (R) and the maximum stock level (S). The formulae for

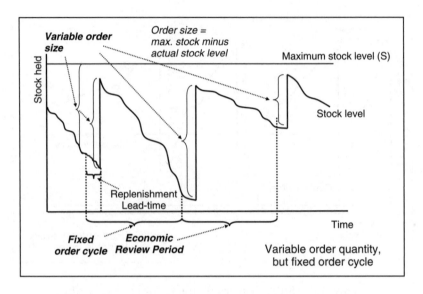

Figure 5.5 Stock control using a reorder cycle policy

these are as follows:

No. of reviews per year

$$r = \sqrt{\frac{A\,i\,Cm}{2\,Co}} \qquad \text{therefore } R = 52/r \text{ (weeks)} \\ \text{or } 12/r \text{ (months)}$$

$$S = A(R+L) + K\sigma\sqrt{(R+L)}$$

The operation of a reorder cycle policy system is shown in Figure 5.5.

Statistical inventory control in practice

The reorder level and reorder cycle policies have a number of comparative advantages and disadvantages connected with them in practice. These are given in Figure 5.6. Both forms of statistic stock control policy, however, have been exposed as having further limitations. To illustrate this, consider the distinction

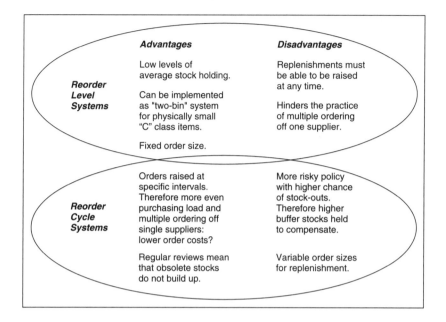

Figure 5.6   Comparison of ROL versus ROC

between products that have 'independent' and 'dependent' demand patterns. Items are said to have independent demand where orders for their replenishment do not depend upon the demand for any other item (e.g. the finished product and spares). Where demand does depend upon higher level items, including components, subassemblies and raw materials, are said to have dependent demand. Some forms of requirements planning (e.g. MRP) are more effective for the purchasing and stock control of items with dependent demand.

Materials requirements planning (MRP)

An MRP system comprises a number of separate modules which integrate to form the overall planning package. The modules include the following

The Master Production Schedule (MPS)

The MPS is a management commitment to produce certain volumes of finished products in particular time periods into the future. This should not be confused with a sales forecast.

The Bill of Material (BOM)

The BOM is, in effect, the parts breakdown or 'recipe' for a finished product. It usually consists of the 'Product Structure File', which holds details of parts and materials that make up each finished product, and the 'Product Master File', holding details concerning parts numbers, unit of measurement, lead-time for procurement/manufacture, etc.

The Inventory Status File

The 'stock file' which keeps a record of all stock balances and transactions. Thus it holds information on the location and condition of materials.

The MRP algorithm

The calculation module which takes information contained in the MPS, BOM and inventory status files and converts these into output reports which detail the planned times for order materials, or for initiating their manufacture in satisfying the production schedule for the finished product. Figure 5.7 illustrates the basic interaction between components of an MRP system.

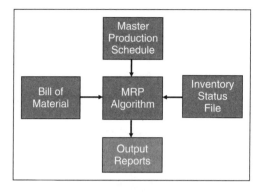

Figure 5.7   Relationship between MRP modules

Operation of an MRP system

The MRP algorithm operates by taking the master production schedule, relating this to the bill of materials file and thus generating gross requirements for each component or raw material. These requirements are then compared with the amount outstanding in stock by reference to the inventory status file so that net requirements (to make or to order) can be determined. Finally, these requirements are offset by the lead-times involved in order to arrive at the planned start times at which to initiate manufacture or purchase of materials. This operation is illustrated schematically in Figure 5.8.

MRP in practice

So far we have considered MRP with the assumption that exact requirements are ordered at distinct points in time. In practice this is over-simplistic: for example ordering quantities may

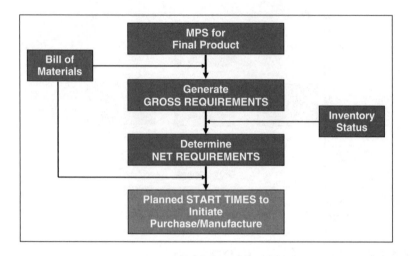

Figure 5.8   The MRP calculation process

need to be in batched units, for example in tens or dozens, etc. Additionally there may be problems of scrap rates and the set-up times on machines. These complications can be taken into account by the operation of variations of the basic MRP programme.

Batch sizing is possible within the operation of an MRP system through the incorporation of a series of rules. These include:

- 'fixed quantity' rules, where ordering is only allowed in quantities of specific increments;

- 'fixed period coverage' rules, where order times are specified and the materials for the next order period are batched and ordered together thus reducing costs of repetitive small ordering; and

- complex 'dynamic' rules, for example where total least cost is the objective and so a programme dynamically calculates requirements and order times by balancing out ordering and holding costs.

The setting of safety stocks to avoid the risk of stockouts is also viable within MRP. These can be set in terms of:

- fixed quantities;
- safety times; and
- percentage increase in requirements (scrap rates).

Manufacturing Resources Planning (MRPII)

MRP deals with materials aspects of operations control. MRPII, however, takes control a stage further by considering the resources available. It therefore recognizes when a materials requirements plan is infeasible (e.g. production schedules generated are greater than capacity) and takes measures to remedy this. MRPII integrates computer control of materials with other areas of computerization within the business including Finance, Marketing, Sales, Design and Engineering, to name a few. MRP II is often seen as closing the control feedback loop by constant monitoring and upgrading of the business's computer-based systems. MRPII, then, is not a newer version of MRP. Rather, MRP forms the material control module of an MRPII system, whereas MRPII is concerned with the effective operation and control of the wider manufacturing system.

The latest progress in this field has seen the development of Distribution Requirements Planning (DRP) and Enterprise Resources Planning (ERP). DRP applies MRP logic to the total supply or logistics chain; it schedules the purchase and movement of material through the supply chain and therefore extends MRP-type control to all types of internal/external stock transactions. This in turn has led to the advent of Enterprise Resources Planning (ERP), which plans how the business resources (materials, employees, customers etc.) are acquired and moved from one state to another.

Summary

The first section of this chapter reviewed the main concepts and techniques of operations planning and control. The theory of control was introduced and then the topics of capacity management and scheduling (including OPT) were discussed. The section illustrated that operations planning and control can be a highly complex process, with a myriad of decisions, options and variables that may influence or disrupt operations plans. It has been illustrated how the use of heuristics can be used to assist the planner in arriving at *reasonable* solutions to capacity and scheduling problems.

The second section covered inventory management in detail. Classical stock control theory using the notion of economic order quantities shows the relationship between demand, costs of ordering, costs of stockholding and service levels. EOQ theory provides the basic principles for inventory management. It was demonstrated how MRP and broader enterprise resources planning can be used in situations of dependent demand, and how it more effectively manages inventory than simple reorder level or reorder cycle inventory systems. Controlling enterprise resources though effective inventory movement and the efficient management of working capital in the business is the 'life blood' of the organization.

Example – Scheduling

'Wood turning business with about a two million pounds turnover. The issue here was they were planning the manufacturing within a spreadsheet and each job was manually input onto the spreadsheet. Because of this, they knew how many hours each machine had loaded, but they didn't for each individual order, they knew the total hours for

each machine, but they didn't actually know when that needed to be dispatched. Another issue was that the salesman didn't know how what he sold affected manufacturing. Communication and real data were a problem here.

So what we did was we looked at putting in a manufacturing planning system which allowed them to manage the production. It actually looked at the machine loadings so that the Manufacturing Manager could increase the capacity via extra shifts (overtime) or eventually by buying new machines. This led to a better production flow and with the manufacturing planning system in place it also allowed them to reduce the stock held by 40 %.'

Example – Inventory Planning and Control

'My company had a base in the Philippines and was awarded some business worth around 50 million pesos a year, so at the time with those exchange rates it was about $1 million per year. This was to do the warehousing for a well known sportswear brand.

This sportswear brand had previously used a distributor to distribute their goods in the Philippines and they had decided to buy and then set-up their own shop. They did not buy the infrastructure of the distributor, the distributor had its own warehouse and its own logistics and infrastructure. We tried to work it so that we didn't have to outsource the warehousing and distribution and the inbound logistics side for their product, but for many reasons this was not feasible.

The company this outsourced contract was awarded to actually received three months' worth of stock in one go. This was pre-season stock prior to them actually going live and distributing the stock. Once they had received the stock off the containers, they then proceeded to put each carton into four bay deep warehouse racking. Unfortunately they mixed up all of the stock, not realizing that there were colour and size combinations.

Three months after they started to receive stock they got the first order. It said 'we want to have this style in black and size seven and we want three pairs of them'. So then there was the problem of having to go through three months' worth of stock to try and find this but there was no WMS (Warehouse Management System) in place, there was nothing. So it really was a case of throwing people at the problem and they employed about 120 extra people to walk around the warehouse with tickets and find stock.

I was sent in to fix the problem and I couldn't actually believe that this had happened. The first thing we did was try to identify the quick fixes. We identified the picking tickets that were outstanding, we tried to identify the fast moving product, because not all of it would be fast moving. So we did a very basic ABC analysis based on velocity and not upon the value, it was quite difficult to do that. And then, because it was a new warehouse, we had quite a lot of space in the warehouse, so we moved all the 'A Stock' and arranged it in style rows and then put colour rows and then arranged it by size. This in time saved at least 66% in terms of space and about three hundred thousand dollars in operating costs.'

Further reading

- Brown, S. (1996) *Strategic Manufacturing for Competitive Advantage*, Prentice Hall, Hemel Hempstead.

- Brown S, Lamming R., Bessant J., and Jones P. (2005) *Strategic Operations Management*, 2nd edn, Butterworth Heinemann, Oxford

- Forrester, J.W. (1961) *Industrial Dynamics*, MIT Press.

- Goldratt, E.M and Cox, J. (1984) *The Goal: Excellence in Manufacturing*, North River Press, New York.

- Kim, B. (2005) *Supply Chain Management*, John Wiley & Sons, Ltd.

- Kornafel, P. (2004) *Inventory Management and Purchasing: Tales and Techniques from the Automotive Aftermarket*, First Books Library.

- Kraut, R., Chan, A., Butler, B. and Hong, A. (1998) *Coordination and Virtualisation: the role of electronic networks and personal relationships. Journal of Operations Management*, 2nd edn, Elsevier Butterworth-Heinemann, Oxford.

- Shingo, S. (1989) *A Study of Toyota Production Systems*, Productivity Press.

- Stevenson, W.J. (2009) *Operations Management*, 10th edn, McGraw-Hill.

- Waters, D. (2002) *Operations Management: Producing Goods and Services*, 2nd edn, FT Prentice Hall.

- Waters, D. (2004) *Inventory Control and Management*, 2nd edn, John Wiley & Sons, Ltd.

Useful internet sites

- www.inventoryops.com Links to inventory articles and organizations.

- www.cips.org The Chartered Institute for Purchasing and Supply.

- www.ism.ws Institute for Supply Management.

- www.supply-chain.org The Supply Chain Council.

- www.oracle.com Oracle, business software company.

- www.sap.com SAP, business software company.

- www.goldratt.com The Goldratt Institute.

- www.toyota.co.uk Detailed information on world car production.

Useful academic journal articles

- Evans, P. and Wurster, T.S. (1997) Strategy and the new economics of information, *Harvard Business Review,* September–October, 71–82.

- Maister, D.H. (1975) Centralisation of Inventories and the square root law, *International Journal of Physical Distribution,* 6(3), 124–34.

- Murray, E.A. and Mahon, J.F. (1993) Strategic alliances: gateway to the New Europe? *Long Range Planning,* 26(4), 102.

- Susaki, T. (1993) What the Japanese have learned from strategic alliances. *Long Range Planning,* 26(6), 41–53.

6 DEVELOPING LEAN OPERATIONS

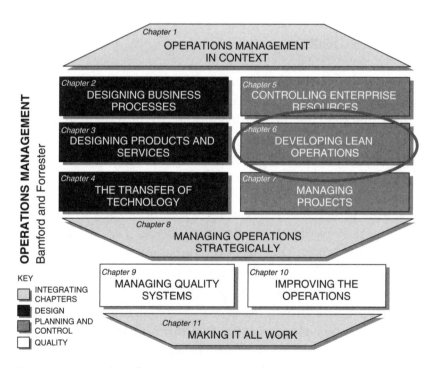

Conceptual model of operations management

Introduction

In recent years increasing attention has been paid to alternative methods of operations planning and control. 'Just-in-time' management (JIT) and lean were widely adopted by Japanese companies and for many years provided them with a distinct competitive advantage. This chapter outlines both philosophies and the techniques employed. Following an introduction to lean the methods of 'pull' logistics management, of which JIT is one form, will be compared with the 'push' systems. The JIT concept, techniques for internal and supply just-in-time management will then be outlined. The section concludes with a more general discussion of contemporary lean supply chain management.

What is 'lean'

Lean involves removing waste, e.g. analogy with the human body: slimmed down, fit and healthy. Waste is defined as 'anything other than the minimum amount of equipment, materials, parts, space, and worker's time, which are absolutely essential to add value to the product' (Shoichiro Toyoda, Chairman, Toyota, 1992–1999).

The lean principles were outlined for the West by Womack, Jones and Roos in 1991 with their book, *The Machine That Changed the World*. They were of course referring to the motor car and the book discussed: the History of Automotive Production; the Principles of Lean Production; Implementing Lean Production. The principles of lean were identified under four headed chapters: Designing the Car; Running the Factory; Dealing with Suppliers; Dealing with Distributors. This book started a drive towards increased efficiency within the West; firstly in the manufacturing sector and now increasingly within the services sector.

Lean is therefore a strategy for remaining competitive by identifying and eliminating wasteful steps in products and processes, using the following practices:

- improvement of equipment reliability;

- quality at the source;

- continuous flow production;

- pull production;

- continuous improvement.

The term 'lean' is used because lean operations use less: human effort; space; capital investment; materials; time between the customer order and delivery. The basic goal is to get more done with less by: minimizing inventory at all stages of production; shortening cycle times from raw materials to finished goods; eliminating all sorts of waste. Types of waste are roughly defined as: overproduction; waiting; transportation; inefficient processing; inventory; unnecessary motion; product defects.

'Push' versus 'pull' logistics

Statistical Stock Control (Reorder Level/Reorder Cycle) and Material Requirements Planning (MRP) Stock Systems are used for processes which operate in 'push' mode. In such purchasing and inventory control systems, order times and anticipated start times are planned and executed in expectation of future demand. In contrast there are now a number of inventory (or usage) based systems defined as 'pull' systems. In these, orders are placed when stocks of parts at the succeeding stage of production reach a predetermined level. Thus, a triggering effect occurs. The adoption of systems which pull requirements from preceding activities only when materials are required is now viewed as an effective way of ensuring manufacturing operations are responsible to market demands. Just-in-time (JIT) systems are the most common form of pull system in operation today.

The JIT concept

JIT is not merely a stock control technique and cannot be bought 'off-the-shelf'. Rather it is a wide-ranging philosophy of waste removal on a continuous path towards 'manufacturing excellence'. It concentrates on improvement as opposed to conventional Western approaches that strive for optimization (e.g. of cost). One of the wastes attacked is stock. Inventory is not seen as an asset, but as excess that serves to hide the causes of root problems. Figure 6.1 provides an example of what is revealed when the levels of inventory are reduced (unreliable supplier deliveries; defective components; poorly coordinated processes). This actually creates the opportunity and provides the focus needed to improve these areas within the operation, thereby creating a more efficient, effective and potentially more profitable operation. JIT originated in Japan and demands high quality, on-time delivery and cost reductions. It is, therefore,

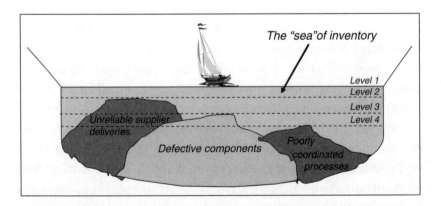

Figure 6.1   The JIT pond analogy (adapted from Singo, 1996)

indicative of many of the contemporary ideas on the role of manufacturing currently prevailing.

A stock control policy based upon JIT suggests the supply of materials to each stage of production when, and only when, required (not before or after). Use of materials at any stage creates a need for materials from the previous stage. This implies that no inventories are held in advance of requirements or in expectation of future demand, but in practice there will always be an element of buffering in a JIT or any other system. When implemented, JIT results in a 'pull' mode of operation of the type described above.

'Push' stock systems are liable to assume certain values when setting parameters for their operation including costs of ordering, lead-times/set up times and holding costs. JIT, in contrast, actively attacks these assumptions and any other problems which prevent synchronization of the operating system and so encourage manufacture or purchase in large batch sizes. There exists much confusion over the use of the term JIT and what it should encompass. It is best thought of as functioning in two discrete, but related, areas: in-house (internal) inventory management and the management of supplier deliveries. Common approaches to each of these facets of JIT will now be presented.

Internal JIT systems

The most widely known and publicized operations control system is existence today is the Toyota 'kanban' system for in-house JIT. Kanban has been used within Toyota's operations departments for many years. A kanban is a card which accompanies parts through a particular stage of the production process. When parts are used, the kanban is returned to the previous process and acts as a signal or trigger for the supply of more material. The number of kanbans in circulation directly controls the amount of stock held. Two types of kanban cards are used by Toyota: the 'production' kanban and the 'conveyance' kanban. Production kanbans are used within an area to initiate a manufacturing operation, whereas conveyance kanbans are used between areas to authorize the movement of materials from one place to another. Applications in other companies have seen the card replaced, with the materials containers acting as triggers (an empty container means it needs to be filled).

JIT supply

The art of JIT supply management is ensuring that just enough material arrives from suppliers at precisely the right time: not too early as this results in high stocks, and not too late as this would disrupt and possibly stop production. Typically JIT supply management involves giving suppliers tight and fairly rigid schedules, but with a very short time horizon (i.e. requirements for the next day rather than the next month). The supplier is then expected to deliver in small batches on a frequent basis to ensure just-in-time and 'just enough' material deliveries. In some companies, most notably in the car industry, a number of final assembly plants have integrated supplier operations into their own internal kanban systems. Thus, a card returned from the vendor, or the receipt of an empty container, acts as a trigger for the supplier to manufacture and/or ship more material. The use of JIT links supposes a very close association between vendor and supplier. To summarize, these objectives are often achieved by: reducing the number of suppliers; reducing the delivery order sizes; and increasing the frequency of deliveries. Supply chains are therefore characterized by long term relationships and a commitment from both parties to work together in the improvement of operations, rather than against one another as is frequently the case in Western industries where vendors are known to issue threats and ultimatums to suppliers.

Continuous improvement and quality

The use of JIT in a company is usually inextricably linked to programmes of quality management through continual improvement. JIT sees inventory as a root of evil, which contradicts the view of inventory as an asset (on the profit and loss account). In JIT, excessive inventory in a system is seen as being indicative of fundamental problems and inefficiencies; it is seen as hiding the problems that exist. It is useful here to refer to the commonly used 'pond' analogy' (see Figure 6.1) which illustrates the issue of excessive stockholding and how JIT can be used to identify and tackle key problems. Inventory in the analogy is seen as being a 'sea', the higher the stockholding the higher the water level. The stock level, however, covers a whole host of problems illustrated as 'rocks' in the analogy. By gradually lowering the water level through inventory reductions one can then uncover problems as they occur: the largest problems become apparent first as these will be the larger rocks. When a problem is discovered, the organization must then switch into problem solving mode and attempt to remove it, or reduce it in size. When this is done the inventory level can be reduced again and the next problem identified and solved.

This objective of JIT fits well with business quality management drives through continual improvement. As such JIT and quality management must be viewed as complementary in the development and improvement of manufacturing operations.

Implementing JIT

Organizations, particularly those in the West, have experienced problems when attempting to implement JIT. The following are just a few of the problems encountered which need serious consideration when implementing JIT. Firstly the practice of bulk purchasing and safety stocks continues to have great attractions for price reductions and contingency management, but runs contrary the JIT philosophy. Secondly, lengthy changeovers serve to justify the continuance of batch production. Therefore JIT has more commonly been implemented for assembly operations and not for preceding operations. Finally materials from outside must be available at short notice with lead-times. This causes severe problems unless suppliers and vendors are extremely well coordinated and able to communicate and respond efficiently. As a result, JIT suppliers tend to be local suppliers and quite commonly are forced to hold stocks for the vendor to draw from.

The question arises whether the stockholding is just being pushed back down the supply chain. Having considered issues such as those above, there exist a number of approaches one may adopt when implementing JIT. For internal JIT these include:

1. Improve product quality and reduce the number of defects.

2. Reduce set-up times on machines to allow for lower cost, more frequent machine changeovers.

3. Reduce batch sizes when manufacturing or assembling products and so reduce work-in-progress.

4. Locate inventories in identifiable areas and then set about reduction.

When adopting JIT for supplier deliveries the following means may be used:

1. Buy from fewer outlets by reducing supplier base.

2. Reduce the delivery sizes of incoming batches.

3. Increase the frequency of deliveries to compensate for (2).

4. Establish long term relationships (partnerships) with suppliers and work with them, not against them, for the purpose of continual improvement.

Supply Chain Management

In recent times managers have sought to develop total systems approaches to ensure a smooth and controlled flow of information, materials and services through the entire supply chain. Supply Chain Management is defined as the set of activities concerned with the design, planning and control of the system which manages the transmission of materials, parts, products and services into, through and out of the organization. It therefore comprises supply channels (inbound logistics) and distribution to customers (outbound logistics). Both are critical in managing the 'value chain' of the business (those areas where the transformation takes place and value is actually created).

Make or buy decisions are information decisions for any organization. Outsourcing, where products and services are bought-in from outside parties, is now an increasingly common practice. Organizations outsource when they decide to purchase something they had been making in-house. In terms of determining which items to buy-in, it is now commonplace to outsource all activities that do not directly represent/support core competencies – firms focus on where they most effectively add value. The bought-in component need not be restricted to physical materials: consider for example the commissioning of consultancy services, assigning suppliers with design responsibility, and the use of turnkey suppliers for developing new facilities.

The 'Value Chain' is a useful concept to refer to when determining supply chain strategies (see Michael Porter, 1985, Competitive Advantage: Creating and Sustaining Superior Performance). Operations and supply strategies are determined by deciding how manufacturing, service and logistics activities are distributed geographically. Value chain analysis provides an indication of where international competitiveness might be generated. It can indicate where the distinctive order winning properties of a firm's product might be developed, and provides guidance for facility/location decisions.

Outsourcing is a common phenomena when the business is seen as being too highly vertically integrated; or when seeking to reduce staff levels (lower costs and increase flexibility); or when there is a desire to increase return on capital employed (ROCE). There are related dangers, though. High levels of outsourcing can result in a reduction in organizational knowledge/skills, a resultant loss of distinctive competencies, hidden costs such as the redesign of systems and the ongoing overheads of managing supply. The rule of thumb, therefore, is that outsourcing should only be done for strategic reasons, not merely for short term cost reductions.

Understanding the transportation network and infrastructure is essential for supply chain/logistics managers. There are many modes of transportation for products including road, rail, ocean/airfreight, pipeline, etc. In making the choice of mode or, more precisely, which combination of modes to use, decisions should be guided by the predictability of the mode, the cost of transportation, and other factors such as environmental friendliness, etc.

Finally it is important to note the influence of E-business trends on supply chain management. The integration of supplier-customer information systems from modern communication technologies has enabled increased benefits for effective supply chain management such as tight control, quick response, efficient response to customer requests, improved marketing communications and relationship management, and faster (including electronic) delivery of goods and services.

Lean and the MIT research project

Between 1985–1990 the Massachusetts Institute of Technology (MIT) conduced the 'International Motor Vehicle Program' (IMVP) on the Future of the Automobile Industry. $5 million in funding was provided from car companies, component suppliers and governments and an international research team of 55 people were involved. They visited 90 assembly plants and hundreds of component supply factories worldwide. Their main observation was that of a worldwide trend from mass to lean production methods. Twice now the auto industry has changed basic ideas about how to manufacture products. The transition from: 'craft' to 'mass' (Fordism) and then 'mass' to 'lean' (Japanization).

The core concepts of lean can be summarized below.

Running the operations

Lean operations equals a lean organization and the main principles of this are: transfer the maximum number of tasks and responsibilities to those people actually adding value in operations; have in place a system for detecting defects and inefficiencies that quickly traces every problem, once discovered, to its ultimate root cause; implement dynamic work teams and widespread multi-skilling (manual, clerical, and problem solving tasks); engender an air of reciprocal obligation – managers must be seen to value skilled workers.

Lean design

To succeed in the design phase there are four key aspects: (i) Leadership: the 'large project leader' with defined responsibility;

(ii) Teamwork: the tightly knit team; (iii) Communication: the ability to solve critical problems early on; (iv) Simultaneous Development: of both products and processes.

Lean supply management

The key facets of lean supply have a great deal in common with JIT: involve suppliers early on in the product design process; devolve responsibility for design; establish prices and analyse costs jointly: use 'market-minus' rather than 'supplier-cost-plus' pricing systems; use value engineering, value analysis and Kaizen to reduce costs in design and over the life cycle of the product/component; use JIT methods for ordering and inventory control in the supply chain; suppliers to assume responsibility for quality.

Dealing with customers in lean operations

Three key aspects exist regards the customers: (i) Brand Loyalty: engage in active, not passive, selling; (ii) Customer Information: treat the buyer as an integral part of the manufacturing process and its information systems (the use of information technology); (iii) Distribution Systems: ensure the system is lean in terms of inventory. In lean organizations the distribution system typically contains only three to four weeks' supply of finished goods, most of which are already sold.

Agile manufacturing

The evolution from 'craft' to 'mass', then 'mass' to 'lean' has paved the way for the beginnings of a 'lean' to 'agile' transformation. This latest trend within manufacturing has been brought about largely through advances in technology. Businesses now have the ability to communicate up and down the supply, operations and distribution networks very quickly. This capability to quickly share and then react to customer needs and market changes, whilst simultaneously controlling quality and costs can provide a distinct competitive advantage. Agile manufacturing is seen as the next step after lean in the evolution of efficient operations.

Summary

This chapter has illustrated the importance of inventory management, not merely due to cost considerations, but also in terms of the strategic effectiveness of operations. In addition to showing the tools and techniques of JIT and lean, the link between practice and the concept of continuous improvement has been shown. Furthermore the chapter has examined the impact of modern forms of supply chain management. Supply chain management involves the timely and cost effective delivery of high quality materials, parts, products and services. 'Intelligent' supply chain management is a source of strategic advantage not only for the cost leader, but also for those businesses seeking to differentiate their activities from competitors by clever use of the value chain. This includes effective means of outsourcing, the application of JIT/lean concepts to supply, and the development of supportive supplier partnerships. It was also noted that selecting the most appropriate modes of transportation is important and should not be neglected or underestimated. Finally E-business has had a profound effect upon the efficiency of supply chain management in recent years. Finally the concept of Agile manufacturing was introduced.

Example – Just-in-Time

'This example is the supply side JIT re-design of a major computer manufacturing plant. What actually occurred in that plant was the manufacture of mainframe computers, but also some assembly operations fed into the final assembly operation. In the implementation of Just-in-Time most people think of it as being zero stock, but in fact, what Just-in-Time should be about is minimizing stock and having it available to respond, but in low levels in identifiable areas. So what the company did was move away from bulk storage at workstations producing wiring harnesses for things such as the AC Motors. They supplied everything in kit form, so that when the demand came from final assembly for supply of more components, that would 'trigger' back to the store system and that would send the kit to produce either one or a small quantity of that product at the workstation.

The key point here is that Just-in-Time is not just about operating with minimum stock, which if most companies operated with minimum stock they would never respond to changes in demand. It is about operating small or low levels of stock in tactical, identifiable, areas and also operating in a pull mode, where demand pulls through rather than being pushed through as in other planning and control systems.'

Example – Outsourcing Strategies

'The company I work for is in the global automotive sector with a number of divisions. The business decided that they needed to outsource its warehousing facilities; this was done very, very quickly and over a short period of time. The rumour was they did it because they wanted a better "sales *to employee" ratio. Outsourcing would therefore take the people out of the business.*

It was all done very quickly and the contract gave the 'power' to the contractor. The business thought that they were going to make a considerable amount of savings but eventually they ended up paying about 30 % more than their original internal warehousing budget to the contractor. This obviously came directly out of our profit. The problem was they hadn't measured the subcontractor in the same way as they did with the original warehouses, if they had done that they would have got much more profit back into the business. That's a typical example of making a strategic supply decision that can actually backfire.'

Further reading

- Bicheno, J. (1991) *Implementing Just-in-Time*, IFS.

- Bicheno, J. (2004) *The New Lean Toolbox: Towards Fast, Flexible Flow*, PICSIE Books, Buckingham.

- Bicheno, J. (2008) *The Lean Toolbox for Service Systems*, PICSIE Books.

- Drew, J., McCallum, B. and Roggenhofer, S. (2004) *Journey to Lean: Making Operational Change Stick*, Palgrave Macmillan, Basingstoke.

- Keyte, B. and Locher, D. (2005) *The Complete Lean Enterprise: Value Stream Mapping for Administration and Office Processes*, Productivity Press.

- Ohno, T. (1988) *Toyota Production System: Beyond Large-Scale Production*, Productivity Press.

- Parry, S., Barlow, S. and Faulkner, M. (2005) *Sense and Respond: The Journey to Customer Purpose*, Palgrave Macmillan, London.

- Russell, R.S. and Taylor, B.W. (2005) *Operations Management*, 5th edn, John Wiley & Sons, Inc.

- Schonberger, R. (2008) *World Class Manufacturing: The Lessons of Simplicity Applied*, Free Press, New York.

- Schonberger, R.J. (1987) *World Class Manufacturing: Implementing JIT and TQC*, Free Press, New York.

- Shingo, S. (1996) *Quick Changeover for Operators: The SMED System*, Productivity Press.

- Womack, J.P. and Jones, D.T. (2007) *Lean Solutions: How Producers and Consumers Achieve Mutual Value and Create Wealth*, Simon & Schuster.

- Womack, J.P., Jones, D.T. and Roos, D. (2007) *The Machine that Changed the World*, Free Press.

Useful internet sites

- www.lean.org Lean Enterprise Institute.
- www.nummi.com New United Motor Manufacturing Inc (General Motors Corporation and Toyota Motor Corporation).
- www.shingoprize.com Shingo Prize for Excellence in Manufacturing.
- www.toyota.com Toyota UK.

Useful academic journal articles

- Krafcik, J.F. (1988) Triumph of the lean production system. *Sloan Management Review*, Fall, 41–52.

- Lodge, A. and Bamford, D. (2008) Using lean techniques in radiology waiting time improvement: a case study, *Public Money and Management*, **28**(1), 49–52.

- Soriano-Meier, H. and Forrester, P.L. (2002) A Model for Evaluating the Degree of Leanness of Manufacturing Firms, *Integrated Manufacturing Systems*, **13**(2), 104–9.

- Womack, J.P. and Jones, D.T. (2005) Lean consumption. *Harvard Business Review*, March, 1–11.

7 MANAGING PROJECTS

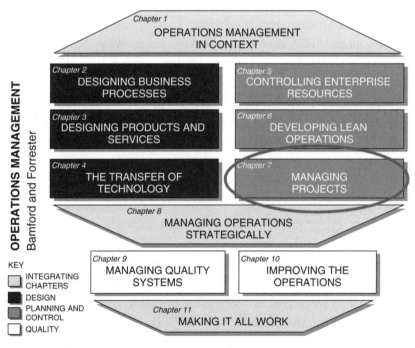

Conceptual model of operations management

Introduction

Project management is an important area of competence for an Operations Manager. The design and introduction of a new process or operations system, and the introduction of a new project, demand skills in terms of managing large projects. Project management is also necessary when introducing a programme of change in work methods or quality management in the improvement of operations. Many large scale projects are the core business of some organizations – e.g. the activities of construction companies, shipbuilders and installers of networked computer systems. A project can be described as a set of activities that has a defined start point and end state. It can be large or small scale, but it is with the former that we are principally concerned here. Large projects are complex, require large quantities of resources, have many internal and external interactions, and are invariably difficult to manage. This section will consider the three main stages in the management of a project: (i) planning; (ii) scheduling; and (iii) control. It will then outline some of the organizational issues frequently encountered in the management of projects, before discussing the role and responsibilities of the project manager.

Project planning

Project planning is a necessary requisite to successful project management. This initial stage of the process involves setting project objectives and, in general terms, determining the terms of reference for the project. It is important from the outset to develop a clear project brief similar to the brief discussed within Chapter 3 on Product and Service Design. The scope of the project should be determined, and the resources necessary to accomplish the project estimated. At this stage the project team should be organized and the responsibilities of team members determined. A rough estimation of time and cost of project activities should also be considered (rough because there will be a great many 'unknowns' at this stage, but an estimate is required for planning purposes). Generally the triangle of factors – time, cost and quality – should be considered and the likely trade-offs between these determined.

Project scheduling

Scheduling is a very important stage of project management. It involves the detailed allocation of resources in the form of people, finance and equipment to activities. Scheduling continues as the project progresses, as there will be a need for regular updating of the schedule as the project commences. Project scheduling often involves the use of project management tools such as Gantt charts and network analysis tools, such as Critical Path Method (CPM) and Programme Evaluation and Review Technique (PERT).

The 'Gantt' chart is the most common form of project scheduling and has been traditionally used in connection with planning and controlling projects. See Figure 7.1 for an example.

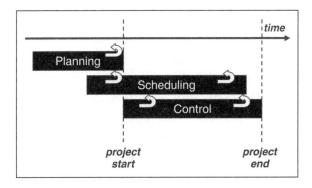

Figure 7.1   Simplistic Gantt chart

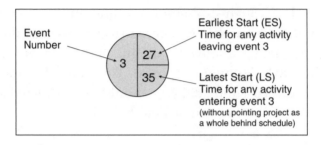

Figure 7.2   Activity on arrow information

However, it is simplistic and does not show the dependency of one activity on another, it cannot be used to identify critical activities and the extent to which other activities can be moved. Resource planning cannot easily be achieved using Gantt charts.

Network planning and analysis techniques overcome the weaknesses associated with Gantt charting and are effective for planning complex projects. There are a number of different variations on the basic network planning approach, including Critical Path Method (CPM) and Programme Evaluation and Review Technique (PERT). There are two basic types of network: 'Activity on Arrow' where an activity is represented by an arrow and the nodes at the beginning and end of the arrow are events; and 'Activity on Node' where an activity is represented by a node and the arrows between nodes simply indicate dependency. Activity on arrow notation is most commonly used in project networks. One of the routes though the network will be critical – any delay in completing any of the activities along this route will delay the whole project. This critical route or critical path through the network is identified by those activities where the 'Earliest Start Time' = 'Latest Start Time' (see Figures 7.2 and 7.3)

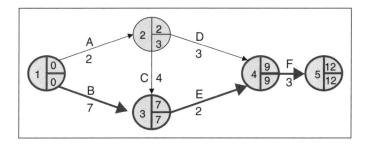

Figure 7.3 Activity on arrow critical path

Program Evaluation and Review Technique (PERT)

This was developed by US Navy and a consulting firm in 1958 for the Polaris submarine project. The technique works in a similar manner to the CPM method, but activity durations have a range of times that follow a statistical distribution. PERT can therefore compute the *probability* of achieving individual activity durations, and project milestones. To do this it uses *beta distribution* and so PERT requires not just expected completion times for activities, but also optimistic and pessimistic estimates (see Figure 7.4). There are six steps in network analysis using CPM and PERT, namely:

1. Define the project and its significant activities and tasks.

2. Develop relationships among activities and decide upon the order/precedence of these.

3. Draw the network.

4. Assign time/cost estimates to activities.

5. Compute the longest path through the network – the critical path.

6. Use the network to schedule and control the project.

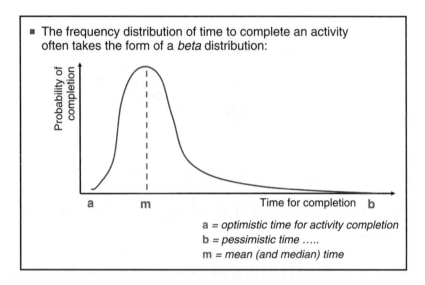

- The frequency distribution of time to complete an activity often takes the form of a *beta* distribution:

a = *optimistic time for activity completion*
b = *pessimistic time .....*
m = *mean (and median) time*

Figure 7.4   Beta distribution for PERT

PERT is a computer-based tool that provides probability-based estimates of completion time as the project proceeds. It also presents details of costs on an ongoing basis, plus information on additional costs of completing activities in reduced times. An additional functionality of PERT is that it can be used as in the post-audit of projects with a view to improving the organization's project management in the future.

Project control

Project control is the third stage of project management, but kicks in at an early stage in the life of a project (when it commences). It involves activities such as monitoring costs, monitoring activity completions and time achievements, monitoring resource usage and people performance, and revising and changing schedules as and when necessary. It must also

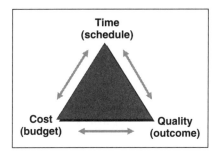

Figure 7.5 The performance triangle – performance objectives and 'trade-offs'

appropriately manage the key project trade-off (cost, quality, and time), see Figure 7.5.

Organizational issues in project management

Projects frequently involve establishing and managing an inter-disciplinary team drawn from across the range of business functions (engineering and design, operations and production, finance, human resources, etc.) in order that appropriate specialist input is provided. This frequently results in some form of matrix management structure to control personnel, with individuals in the team continuing to report to their functional superior in addition to the project team managers. This, however, presents problems in many instances for the project manager. The question arises: 'who, exactly, exerts the main power and influence in such an arrangement?' It is important that the project manager is allowed to exert some degree of influence within the organization and senior managers afford that authority to the project axis in this organizational matrix. Without such authority, the job of the project manager is extremely difficult to accomplish.

Responsibilities of the project manager

As well as authority, project managers have a number of important responsibilities in their role. Some of these are listed below:

1. Thoroughly plan the project and solicit the involvement of functional areas.

2. Control manpower needed by the project.

3. Control basic technical definition of the project, and balance technical versus cost trade-offs.

4. Exercise strong positive leadership.

5. Monitor performance.

6. Complete on schedule and within cost – the project manager's essential performance criteria.

(adapted from Bowenkamp and Kleiner, 1987)

Summary

This section has provided an overview of the important activity of project management. The stages of managing a project have been identified as planning, scheduling and control, and each has been discussed. The use of a number of network analysis project management tools, including CPM and PERT, have been described. Finally the important issues of organizational control, power and politics, and the responsibilities of the project manager have been discussed.

Example – Project Planning Issues

'This is a large engineering corporation with about a £2.4 billion turnover. I was involved in implementing a project *management system which actually managed the introduction of new products. Two divisions I worked with, one was the diesel systems and the other was the aerospace, and they had completely different ways of operating. Diesel systems actually put together a project planning template which went through each stage of the development, which acted for new project managers as a check list. So it would look at things like, do I need to look at any new technology? Do I need to buy and invest in any machinery and things like that? So each stage was dealt with in a fine amount of detail and it meant that we could actually look at what had been missed and assess the risk of each of those.*

Aerospace on the other hand is product manager driven and it was like a small business within a larger business. They didn't have planning templates but each manager actually learnt from his own mistakes. The communication between the project managers or the product managers wasn't as good as it ought to be and therefore they didn't get any synergy between projects, whereas in the diesel systems they did. Therefore within one organization you had two very distinct and different methods, one which was much better than the other, project planning templates, giving you more chance to capture the benefits and to take fewer risks.'

Example – Project Planning Issues

'Many people look at and think of project management as network analysis, critical path approaches, tools and techniques. But in fact it is more than that. An example is an organization I have been working with, a County Council in the UK. I was asked to work with them in terms of introducing project management to the organization. Their main reason though for doing that is not just because project

management is a good idea, it is a good idea to manage your products and projects effectively, but they could see it as part of a culture change within the organization.

Public Sector organizations such as councils and county councils in the UK are often quite bureaucratic, often run operations as routines and don't always manage for outcomes. And, in fact, if we look at what project management is trying to do; it's trying to say there is identifiable start point, some objectives and therefore an ending point or an outcome. So, by introducing people within the County Council to the tools, techniques and approaches of project management, the main driver behind that was to increase efficiency and performance generally of people, and to make them think towards managing the change and managing for outcomes and performance and evaluating the performance of projects that they have been involved with.

So, project management yes – tools and techniques that can be employed and deployed within organizations but importantly it's about the culture of trying to set objectives, trying to identify staff points and also managing for outcomes in terms of time. Time and cost objectives and also quality and outcome.'

Further reading

- Cadle, J. and Yeates, D. (2008) *Project Management/or Information Systems*, 5th edn, Pearson Education, Harlow.

- Hughes, B. and Cotterell, M. (2006) *Software Project Management*, 4th edn, McGraw-Hill.

- Lock, D. (2008) *Project Management*, 9th edn, Gower, Aldershot.

- Nicholas, J.M. and Steyn, H. (2008) *Project Management for Business, Engineering, and Technology: Principles and Practice,* 3rd edn, Elsevier Butterworth-Heinemann, Oxford.

- Sapolsky, H.M. (1972) *The Polaris System Development: Bureaucratic and Programmatic Success in Government,* Harvard University Press, pp. 118–19.

Useful internet sites

- www.pmi.org Project Management Institute.

- www.projectmanagement.com Articles regarding project management.

- www.projectnet.co.uk Project Manager Today.

Useful academic journal articles

- Czuchry, A.J. and Yasin, M.M. (2003) Managing the project management process, *Industrial Management & Data Systems,* **103**(1).

- Ford, D.N. and Bhargav, S. (2006) Project management quality and the value of flexible strategies, *Engineering, Construction and Architectural Management,* **13**(3).

- Haponava, T. and Al-Jibouri, S. (2009) Identifying key performance indicators for use in control of pre-project stage process in construction, *International Journal of Productivity and Performance Management,* **58**(2).

8 MANAGING OPERATIONS STRATEGICALLY

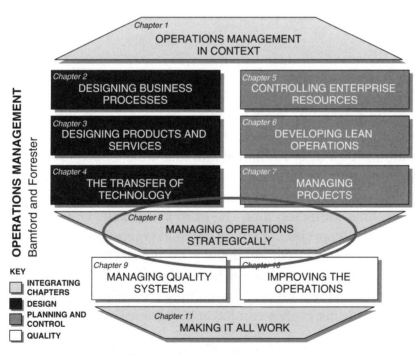

Conceptual model of operations management

Introduction

This book started off by providing a context to Operations Management: a brief history lesson in terms of where it came from. It moved on to cover design aspects then control systems. This chapter will cover: how strategies are actually formulated and what they can do for us; some of the conflicts involved; and some structured approaches to apply them within operations management. How do we manage all this strategically? What does having a strategic edge mean for organizations, what does it mean when it is there in operations?

The chapter reviews existing theory and practice in what has been a developing area of study over the last thirty years. In particular the strategic frameworks provided by Hill, the Cambridge Group and Hayes and Wheelwright are presented and examined.

What is strategy?

The best definition we have come across is: 'A strategy is the total pattern of decisions and actions that position the organisation within its environment and that are intended to achieve its long term goals' (Slack *et al*, 2007, p. 36). It is the *total* pattern, more than just one decision set and it is different disciplines fitting together. The *environment* statement makes it contextually specific, it is about the market sector: service; petrochemical; pharmaceutical; manufacturing; etc. In terms of long term goals, the organization needs to acknowledge what they are and actually understand what long term within their sector actually means; every sector has at least some knowledge of this.

What is long term? It is different for different sectors, for example: the education sector, five years; the healthcare sector, three years; plastic injection moulding, two to three years; exhibitions organizing, three to five years; pharmaceuticals 10 to 15 years.

The role of strategy in operations management

The operations management function can be either a *'competitive weapon'* or a *'millstone'* for a company; it is seldom neutral (see Skinner, 1978; 1985). Skinner argued that by adopting a strategic approach to managing operations the organization could achieve competitive edge over its rivals. By not paying sufficient attention to the product or service provided and its links with corporate objectives, the operations element can impede corporate success even when corporate objectives have been well stated and an effective marketing strategy has been formulated.

Operations management is short term, from one to 12 months dependent on the market sector. Think of the difference between product life cycles for mobile phones versus cars. The level of analysis is micro, it is a focus on the specific process, the manufacture of tables, the delivery of a service.

Operations strategy is longer term, from one to 10 years dependent on the market sector. The level of analysis is macro, it looks at the entire organization. This is not just a physical boundary; it can be across national boundaries and globally. Think of Virgin Plc; within Sir Richard Branson's empire there are a number of distinct companies.

But why are operations sometimes viewed as having little or no strategic importance? Because operations usually perform defined tasks, they do the transformation bit: they provide the point of service; they make the tables. What they do is immediate; it is visible and happening now. According to Hill (1993) this reactive perception of the role is due to:

- the Operations Managers' view of themselves;
- the organization's view of the operations manager's role;
- operations managers are often too late in the corporate debate;
- the operations managers' lack of business language.

So, as a consequence, operations management input is often omitted in strategy development. Why? Because the operations people do not get invited to the meetings, because they are providing the service, making the tables. They are too busy re-designing and optimizing the 'systems', trying to make them lean and agile, managing difficult suppliers and demanding customers. This all takes a degree of time!

Often the operations management people, their input and expertise, are omitted because the strategic development is done by the senior team and the Chief Executive Officer (CEO). It is done by the people who get paid most: the senior board, the directors, the CEO; they get paid to develop and implement strategy. They have a vested interest to get it right, but also to prove their own worth. Sometimes this means others' opinions are omitted from the decision making process.

Operations, as the key service providers, the 'transformation' people, should have a central role in terms of developing the strategic competitive advantage. Within every successful company they do indeed play a central role.

For a 'strategic difference' in operations, to link marketing and operations, companies need to identify and distinguish between *order-qualifiers* and *order-winners*:

- *Order-qualifying* criteria get a service or product into the market place or on to customers' shortlists and keep it there (conforms to the basic requirements: ability to supply; registration to required quality standards; etc).

- *Order-winning* criteria give the product or service superiority over the offerings of competing organizations.

Typical order qualifiers and winners include: price (cost); design; quality; delivery speed; delivery reliability; demand flexibility; product/service range; colours/patterns; economy of use; design leadership; technical support; after sales service.

Hayes and Wheelwright

Robert Hayes and Steven Wheelwright developed a useful framework intended to provide guidance for managers when attempting to evolve their strategies and operations (Hayes and Wheelwright, 1984). Whilst originally written with the manufacturing sector in mind the premise can be applied equally well to the service sector. The four stages are described below.

Internally neutral: minimize manufacturing's negative potential

Senior managers view the manufacturing function as neutral, that is to say it is incapable of influencing competitiveness success. The emphasis here is to minimize any negative influence that manufacturing may have upon corporate and market developments.

Externally neutral: Achieve parity with competitors

Senior managers see manufacturing as important only in so much as it matches the effectiveness and efficiency of competitors in the same industry. Here the emphasis is upon following industry practices in managing the workforce, avoiding large step innovations in product or process technologies, and viewing economies of scale and efficiency as the most important factors in production.

Internally supportive: Provide credible support to the business strategy

Senior managers expect manufacturing to support and strengthen the company's competitive position. They see the contribution of manufacturing as deriving from and dictated by corporate objectives. They ensure decisions made in manufacturing are consistent with corporate and marketing strategies, that strategy is translated in terms meaningful to manufacturing personnel, and are proactive in developing longer term manufacturing strategies at the functional and factory levels.

Externally supportive: Pursue a manufacturing-based competitive advantage

This is where senior executives see manufacturing capabilities as a significant influence upon overall competitiveness. So manufacturing strategy is not merely determined by internal corporate and marketing strategies, but also allows manufacturing executives to have a meaningful role in contributing to the development of the company and its strategies as a whole. In some cases this will result with the realization that manufacturing is the key competitive weapon within the organization.

Managers can identify at which stage their companies are in this framework and therefore identify changes that need to be made within the organization to progress to the next stage.

Structured approaches to formulating manufacturing strategy

Most of the available advice concerning operations strategy tends to be promotional and highly prescriptive without providing any meaningful structure for the detailed analysis of operations decision making. Two approaches to the analysis and formulation of operations strategy have been produced which provide practical guidelines in the development of strategies. They are Hill's framework (Hill, 2004) and the Cambridge Group's methodology (DTI, 1988).

Hill's framework for analysing manufacturing strategy

Hill summarizes his arguments and discussion within his 'framework for reflecting strategy issues in corporate decisions'. This framework is reproduced in Figure 8.1.

Fundamental to the framework is an understanding of step three 'how products win orders in the market-place'. In turn it is argued that the mix of these comes from two major sources: (i) the customer or market as reflected in corporate strategies; or (ii) from the inherent features of the operation system on the other.

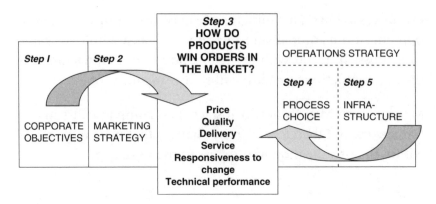

Figure 8.1   Framework for analysing production/operations strategy (adapted from Hill, 2005)

The organization must identify the order-winning criteria for its products; i.e. the correct balance between the factors detailed above, and then reflect these in corporate objectives, market strategy and operations systems design. The five steps in the framework are defined as:

1. Define corporate objectives.

2. Determine marketing strategies to meet these objectives.

3. Assess how different products/services win orders against competitors.

4. Establish the most appropriate mode to manufacture these sets of products or provide these sets of services – process choice.

5. Provide the infrastructure required to support the production/operations process.

The Hill framework demonstrates how market and competitive decisions are, and should be, linked with decisions on operations systems design. Moreover it explores the relationships from the 'bottom-up' and illustrates how excellence in operations can provide order-winning characteristics for services and products which may not have been recognized as winners by corporate decision makers and marketing managers.

The framework can be used in two ways: (i) utilized for the assessment and evaluation of the effectiveness of operations in relation to corporate objectives and product markets; (ii) it serves as a guide for developing new, market-focused strategies and systems in operations. As such it represents a significant contribution to the study of operations strategy and process decisions.

The DTI/Cambridge group methodology

This methodology for developing operations strategy was devised at Cambridge University for the UK Department of Trade and Industry (DTI). It covers such issues as determining market requirements, competitor threats, performance of existing systems, and how to combine all these into a comprehensible and meaningful blueprint. The framework of the methodology is shown in Figure 8.2. A key feature of the methodology is that, through the use of worksheets which the user completes, it not only performs an analysis of the market and competitive environment within which an organization operates, but also conducts an audit of existing operations facilities and competencies. In this way it looks for areas in which system performance may be improved and to better align operations to the market needs. The methodology involves three main phases:

Stage One – generating basic data on product families which
  indicates the importance of the family to the business and
  the strength within current markets. The competitive criteria
  for each family are then determined (e.g. price, delivery
  performance, etc.) and the organization's current
  performance against these criteria is assessed. Finally

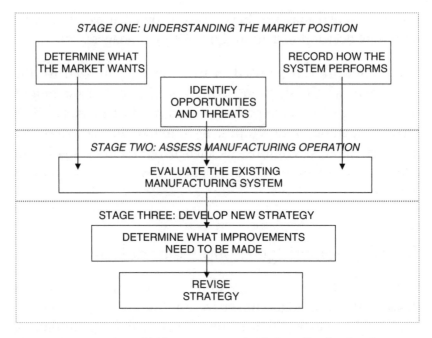

Figure 8.2 DTI/Cambridge group methodology for the development of manufacturing strategy

potential areas of product profitability and vulnerability within the business are identified.

Stage Two – an assessment of current operations strategy and analysis of this in nine areas, namely:

- o *Facilities:* the manufacturing factories, including number, size, location and focus.

- o *Capacity:* the maximum output for each factory.

- o *Span of process:* the degree of vertical integration.

- o *Processes:* the transformation activities and the way they are organized.

- o *Human resources:* the people-related factors.

- o *Quality:* the means of assuring products, processes and people operate to specification.

○ *Control policies:* the operations planning/control guidelines and philosophies of manufacture.

○ *Suppliers:* Relations and methods to ensure delivery of input materials.

○ *New products:* The mechanisms and processes for managing new product introduction.

Stage Three – using the results of the analyses conducted in Stages One and Two and developing a new operations strategy linking operations activities with corporate strategy and market needs. The process steps in this strategy formulation are identified as:

1. Select the most important product families, based upon assessments of the relative contributions to profits, growth potential of market share or overall market size, and current strength within markets.

2. Take each family in turn, compare the market competitive criteria with the achieved performance.

3. Identify the operations policies which contribute to any mismatch between the competitive criteria and the actual performance.

4. Identify the weaknesses of the policies.

5. Consider opportunities and threats.

6. Identify possible actions and strategic choices.

7. Repeat for other families.

In summary, the DTI/Cambridge Group methodology is a means of linking operations systems choices with corporate and marketing strategy. The originators suggest that the methodology can be used in two main ways: (i) for auditing existing operations activities in order to identify current strengths and weaknesses; and (ii) as a framework for reviewing operations strategy and developing a new one if need be. As such, it not only provides a useful insight into the process of operations strategy formulation, but also suggests a practical approach by which organizations might arrive at appropriate strategies for production and market-focused systems development.

Strategy and the product life cycle

Figure 8.3 represents the four distinct stages of the product life. In terms of strategic applications, this is something that needs to be thought through carefully. The strategy adopted at different points in time for products within an organization, makes the difference between companies being successful or not.

Achieving a strategic edge in operations

Hill and the Cambridge Group provide an interesting insight into the activity of strategy formulation and translation. However, they adhere to a top-down and rather overly market deterministic view of operations system development. A further criticism is that they say very little about human resource management (HRM). Modern concepts of HRM are seen as directly influencing quality and service performance. Quality programmes are frequently used as the strategic vehicle to

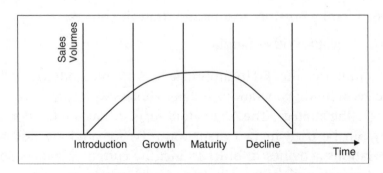

Figure 8.3   The product life cycle

change the attitudes and beliefs of employees, and so enable operational activities to be more market-focused and customer orientated.

Within operations strategies the market-driven approach has led to a partial retreat from traditional scientific management and 'Fordist' techniques which seek to exploit economies of scale, minimize cost and maximize labour productivity. This approach did not place high emphasis upon the notion of continual improvement. Typically optimization of operations was sought, usually to minimize total costs of inventory, but little attempt was made to improve parameters upon which such optimization was based, such as reducing costs of ordering and so lowering the economic order quantity.

The areas in which strategic improvement are sought are numerous; some examples will be given here. There is an obvious progression from macro strategy development to discussions involving specific performance objectives. The performance objectives (or key performance indicators, KPIs) are usually given as:

- Quality – doing things right the first time.
- Speed – doing things fast.
- Dependability – doing things when you say you are going to.
- Flexibility – being able to change what you do.
- Cost – doing things cheaply or at a price the market will bear.

These five, in combination, give us the polar diagram. See Figure 8.4. This can be usefully employed to justify, communicate and legitimize changes in strategy and approach by overlaying the 'footprint' for one company over another.

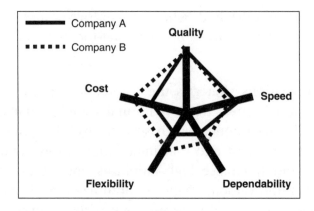

Figure 8.4 Performance objectives polar diagram

Note that each of these independent performance objectives has a distinct relationship with the others. They are inter-dependent: if we want to be the fastest and provide the best quality it is going to increase the cost. This obviously has an impact upon strategic planning and needs to be factored in. At its most basic level it means companies cannot change what they want to because of the consequences involved.

Much attention has been given to the reduction of lead-times in terms of product design; the faster a company can move from the original design specification, to provision of that service or product, the more attractive the item will be to the market. Similarly, short delivery lead-times, from the placing of an order to receipt of the service or goods, will attract customers who, given the choice, prefer delivery sooner rather than later. Much attention has also been given to increasing the level of operational flexibility and widening the range of tasks which can be accomplished within the existing operational systems in order to satisfy the specific and specialized needs of individual customers. Costs remain an important factor because of their direct relation to profit and selling prices. In addition to improved labour productivity, however, much greater importance is now given to the reduction of costs through lowering inventory levels and increasing stock turnovers.

Quality also has an important part to play in the operations strategy of the market-driven company. Quality can be viewed in two different ways: in a product sense and, more holistically, in an organizational context. Quality and reliability is an important attribute for any product and levels of sales are often determined by a company's past reputation in this respect. However, quality in its wider organizational sense is often seen as fundamental in establishing and maintaining the appropriate culture and attitudes within the organization. Total Quality Management and its associated methods and processes are, as a result, now seen as important components of operations strategy.

Summary

This chapter considered the process of operations strategy formulation and has provided guidance upon how this may be conducted. The literature on operations strategy was reviewed and seems to suggest that a strategic, that is to say top-down, and market orientated approach to operations should be taken by managers so that quality and service become integral parts of the strategy alongside factors such as cost and efficiency. The range of services and products required by the market and the response demands in terms of time to market and order response are critical areas in which the company should seek to satisfy its customers. This calls for flexibility within operations to cope with these demands.

Decision makers must understand and analyse the main inputs or key parameters to the process of strategy formulation when developing manufacturing strategy. These criteria include the corporate policy and objectives of the organization, its market strategy, and an internal audit of the competencies within the operations and supporting functions of the business. In so doing an appropriate and realistic strategy can be developed, and from this, strategies for separate operations units can be set. As a final thought it should be acknowledged that operations strategies also have an ethical dimension – business and operations strategy decisions impact communities, regions and sectors. The impact on quality of life issues is something that is increasingly regarded as important.

Example – Manufacturing Strategy

'I was involved in a company which used the Hill Framework. Essentially they were doing an analysis of Corporate Objectives and looking at the marketing strategy and considering the order winners and order qualifiers, but particularly looking at the process and infrastructure improvements they could make to the business.

The company made wiring harness, the large automotive wiring looms that plug into the back of the car dashboard, wiring out to the lights and the electronics. They have always been competing on cost and price, but what the engineers were doing was a project introducing advanced computer integrated manufacturing, really trying to change the way in which they did business and the way in which they supplied information to manufacturing. What this involved was taking electronic drawings directly from customers' computer aided design systems, CAD systems. What that meant was they would very quickly manipulate those and produce changes. This was useful because the vehicle manufacturers, including US and Japanese transplant companies, each year changed designs and so obviously there was a time lag between them deciding on a new design, a change or modification, and the supplier being able to produce the wiring harness to effect that change.

What happened was that sales and marketing were originally competing on price, but with the advances being made through the technology they realized they could respond quicker than the competition. So, they could now take the drawing and produce the new components in eight to 10 weeks rather than it taking four or five months. What this means is that the company, when they actually got talking, the marketing department, the engineers and operations, they realized in fact that the main competitive advantage was in competing on speed.

So what we see here is a good example where the previous model dealing with the manufacturers was based upon price competition whereas they were actually able to compete on speed and flexibility. Much more suitable to the needs of adjusting time, environment, and a low stock environment.'

Example – Strategy Improvement

'We are an international energy company operating in one hundred and thirty five countries, with about one hundred and fifty thousand employees. As part of the business strategy within the company we set-up an internal consultancy to promote best practice within the multiple organizations that make up the total company. We now have internal businesses come to the consultancy and we look into areas of key performance indicators, process mapping, internal and external benchmarking, and generally areas that we can improve in terms of business strategy and processes. It's all linked to the wider business strategy and works very well.'

Example – Distribution Strategy

'The company involved was a distributor for fashion items, footwear, clothing, bags, watches, sunglasses, accessories, etc. The turnover was about eight hundred million dollars. There was an issue bringing footwear from China into Europe, this was around 1999/00. The WTO issues with these are starting to fade out now, but at the time it was a serious issue, bringing footwear from China. China was producing the footwear for about $5 or $6 cheaper per pair, so it was a good opportunity.

The problem was getting the quota in. We had all sorts of issues about how the quota works and things to get around it. But basically what we did, we identified a loop-hole in the quota rules that allowed special technology in the product, so we designed the product to classify as special technology. Then we went and approached various governments in Europe and said to them 'we are going to make a million pairs of these shoes, we are going warehouse them in your country and we are going to distribute and use the infrastructure within your country, we are going to pay duty and we also are going to have assurances in Europe and will be paying VAT', which was then payable back to that government. We talked to a few governments and the Dutch government was actually the easiest to deal with and the most open to this idea. So therefore we got the necessary quotas approved by the government, we signed for a fifty thousand square foot warehouse and distributed to our customers.

It also allowed us to change our terms for our customers from FOB (Freight on Board) to DDP (Delivered Duty Paid), and this is interesting because our customers were paying duty based upon our selling price to them and by changing *the terms it allowed us to pay duty on the selling price, the cost price of the goods, so we actually ended up saving about two million dollars or so on duty. This was a medium term strategic decision taken at the highest level and worked very well.'*

Further reading

- Bennett, D.J. and Forrester, P.L. (1993) *Market-Focused Production Systems: Design and Implementation,* Prentice-Hall, Hemel Hempstead.

- Brown, S., Lamming, R., Bessant, J. and Jones, P. (2005) *Strategic Operations Management,* 2nd edn, Elsevier Butterworth-Heinemann.

- Hayes, R., Pisano, G., Upton, D. and Wheelwright S. (2005) *Operations, Strategy, and Technology: Pursuing the Competitive Edge,* John Wiley & Sons, Ltd.

- Hayes, R.H. and Wheelwright, S.C. (1984) *Restoring Our Competitive Edge: Competing Through Manufacturing,* John Wiley & Sons, Ltd.

- Hayes, R.H., Wheelwright, S.C. and Clark, K.B. (1988) *Dynamic Manufacturing: Creating the Learning Organization,* Free Press, New York.

- Hill, T. (2005) *Operations Management,* 2nd edn, Palgrave Macmillan.

- Hill, T.J. (1993) *Manufacturing Strategy: The Strategic Management of the Manufacturing Function,* 2nd edn, MacMillan, London.

- Johnson, G., Scholes, K. and Whittington, R. (2008) *Exploring Corporate Strategy: Text and Cases,* 8th edn, FT Prentice Hall.

- Porter, M.E. (1985) *Competitive Advantage: Creating and Maintaining Superior Performance*, Free Press, New York.

- Skinner, W. (1978) *Manufacturing in the Corporate Strategy*, John Wiley & Sons, Inc, New York.

- Skinner, W (1985) *Manufacturing: The Formidable Competitive Weapon*, John Wiley & Sons, Inc, New York.

- Slack, N. (1991) *Manufacturing Advantage: Achieving Competitive Manufacturing Operations*, Mercury.

- Slack, N. and Lewis, M. (2008) *Operations Strategy*, 2nd edn, Pearson Education Ltd.

- Slack, N., Chambers, S. and Johnston, R. (2007) *Operations Management*, 5th edn, Pearson Education Ltd.

- Vonderembse, M.A. and White, G.P. (2004) *Core Concepts of Operations Management*, John Wiley & Sons, Ltd.

Useful internet sites

- www.innovateuk.org UK Technology Strategy Board, useful UK resource site on strategy.

Useful academic journal articles

- Brown S., Blackmon K., and Squire, B. (2007) The contribution of manufacturing strategy involvement and alignment to world class manufacturing performance, *International Journal of Operations & Production Management*, 27(3), 282–302.

- Ferdows, K. and de Meyer, A. (1990) Lasting improvements in manufacturing, *Journal of Operations Management*, 9(2), 168–84.

- Fetzinger, E. and Hau, L.L. (1997) Mass customization at Hewlett Packard: the power of postponement. *Harvard Business Review*, 75(1), 116–21.

- Mintzberg, H. and Waters, J.A. (1995) Of strategies: deliberate and emergent. *Strategic Management Journal*, 6(3), 257–72.

- Pine, B., Best, V. and Boynton, A. (1993) Making mass customisation work. *Harvard Business Review*, September–October, 108–19.

- Skinner, W (1969) Manufacturing – Missing Link in Corporate Strategy, *Harvard Business Review*, May–June.

- Skinner, W. (1974) The focused factory. *Harvard Business Review*, May–June, 113–21.

- Teece, D.J. and Pisano, G. (1994) The dynamic capabilities of firms: an introduction. *Industrial and Corporate Change*, 3(3), 537–56.

- Wheelwright, S.C. (1981) Japan: Where Operations Really Are Strategic, *Harvard Business Review*, Vol. 59, July–August.

9 MANAGING QUALITY SYSTEMS

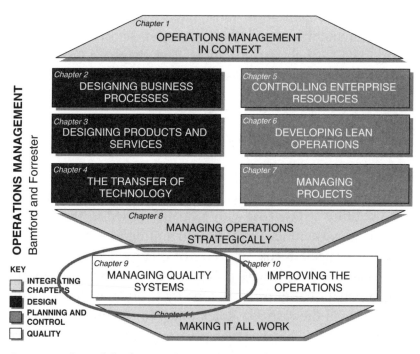

Conceptual model of operations management

Introduction

Definitions and interpretations of what comprises 'quality' vary considerably. In addition, once defined the means by which to best manage quality is open to considerable debate. This chapter sets the scene on various views and dimensions of quality systems management.

At its most basic Quality Control is the measurement of variables or attributes and the use of this data to assess quality of output. It provides an indication of where changes, if any, should be made to processes, procedures, materials and perhaps even the people working in the organization. To aid this a number of statistical methods have been developed and widely adopted since the 1920s; however, these do come with a health warning – before adoption an organization must pay attention to the means of measurement and whether particular statistical tools are appropriate to their circumstances. The chapter considers the tools of quality control and issues identified above.

Definitions of quality

It has been said, 'Good quality does not necessarily mean high quality. It means a predictable degree of uniformity and dependability at low cost with a quality suited to the market' (W. Edwards Deming, 1982). In attempting to adopt an operationally strategic focus on issues of quality it is necessary to appreciate that people have different and often blurred conceptions of what quality really is. Quality is often associated with expense, as in the case of a Rolex watch for example. However, it is quite possible to pay a high price for something and receive inferior goods or to pay a relatively low price in return for something of 'high' quality.

Definitions of quality depend in no small part on the respective market for a particular item and the intended use of the product. It is useful to see quality as a perceived characteristic which varies with each individual, although a fairly common description of quality would be 'fitness for purpose'.

Quality is not simply a matter for manufacturing companies. Service and public sector organizations recognized that quality is central to future business success. Indeed, businesses in general require certain standards of quality of service in order to retain their customers.

Examination of the quality of a product only has purpose when the product is related to its function. So, a brass paper clip could be considered a high quality product for attaching sheets of paper together, but poor quality as a tie-clip. It is useful to consider the quality of a product or service as a function of two specifics:

1. Its specified design.
2. Conformance to this specification.

Traditionally quality assurance systems have been developed where the emphasis has been placed on conformance via the use of 'inspection' and 'testing' procedures, 'quality control' (feeding back quality information for decision making purposes) and 'quality audit' (control of the quality system itself). Techniques for the control of quality conformance tend to be statistical in nature and include 'statistical process control' (SPC) for quality measurement of in-house operations and 'acceptance sampling' for the control of incoming or brought-in items.

Quality assurance via assessment of conformance to design specifications can be viewed as a policy of 'detection'. This can be contrasted with the emphasis within quality systems on the design of the product or service; a 'prevention' policy that is focused on delivering a right-first-time service or product.

Quality systems

When considering the operation of a quality management system, it is useful at a fundamental level to consider it as comprising three levels of measurement and control. These three levels are: (i) inspection; (ii) quality control; and (iii) quality audit (see Figure 9.1).

Level 1 – inspection

Quality inspection comprises the measurement and evaluative activities that take place to assess the quality of incoming and outgoing goods and services at each stage of service delivery or production. It also incorporates 'work-in-progress' (WIP), part-finished service or production inventory. Inspection takes many forms and can involve measuring dimensions, checking weight, measuring performance in some way or else more qualitative

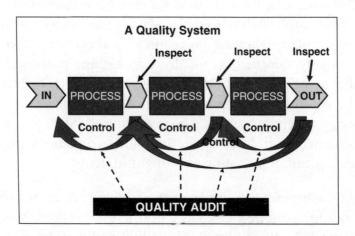

Figure 9.1 Overview of a basic quality system

checks on appearance, perceived views on innate quality, service provision, etc. Inspection by itself is not enough: it is what the organization does with inspection data that is important. Hence the need for the next level in the quality system: quality control.

Level 2 – control

Quality control involves the evaluation of data from quality inspection, identifying any variations to desired standards and then feeding this data back to earlier stages in the production or service process enabling adjustments to be made to materials, processes, procedures and/or people wherever necessary. Control, in the context of quality control, does not fully assure the quality of products or services. The question may arise as to whether the standards are high enough; or the control procedures appropriate; or measuring equipment accurate. It is for these reasons, amongst many others, that the quality inspection and control systems must be periodically audited. This is the next level in the quality system.

Level 3 – audit

Quality audit is, in effect, control of the quality control system. It works at all levels. In its simplest form it can involve the checking and calibration, where necessary, of measurement equipment such as gauges, rulers, weighing machines, weights or computerized programs. It may involve periodic assessment of the use of control data and whether appropriate actions are taken. A high level form of quality audit has developed which is equally applicable to both service and manufacturing sectors, the ISO 9000 Quality System Series. Under this system 'external examiners', or Auditors, of quality control procedures are engaged. If the quality systems in use are deemed satisfactory, i.e. they comply with set International Standards, the organization is awarded an appropriate quality certificate for a set period of time, after which the company will be subject to another review. Sometimes the auditor and award actual come from a specific company, for example L'Oreal, Ford (Q1 and Q101) assessment.

Unfortunately this type of set-up is not efficient, because you employ people to inspect, control and audit, but they are not actually adding any value to the service or product. They are looking for problems or defects that should not have happened anyway. Ideally you should design an efficient process which has a repeatable system built into it for repeatability and productivity; that way you do not need to employ these people, you can take them out and reduce the head count, thereby improving your key ratios. So a tangible way of reducing costs and improving overheads is to remove inspection; a way of doing it is to improve the product quality and the repeatability by designing or re-designing it to produce more 'right first time'.

Most operations and businesses strive for this effect but there are some exceptions. For example, in pharmaceutical production and aircraft manufacture there is lots of inspection because it is safety critical, i.e. planes could fall from the sky if they are made wrong, and so lots of testing takes place. This is part of the reason that planes and pharmaceutical medicine are so very expensive.

International quality standards

Various 'standards' exist for companies to achieve accreditation against. Often the type of standard chosen by companies is specific to the sector within which they operate. For example ISO Standards 9001, 14001, 18001 and 27001. The International Standard Series (ISO 9000) was developed largely on the basis of the British Standard, BS5750. The 1994 version of ISO 9000 had requirements for accreditation contained within a set of 20 criteria ranging from defining specific management responsibility to documents control to handling, storage and delivery of materials (see www.iso.org).

These were designed to be broadly applicable to any organization seeking registration, whether service or manufacturing based. However, the ISO 9000 (1994) series did not strictly deal with: continuous improvement; leadership; people involvement; customer delight; or business results. These were viewed as major weaknesses of the standard and the 2000 revision incorporates two major additions: (i) continuous improvement methods (what and how do companies improve); (ii) resources planning and management (how are resources planned, allocated, managed, and what are the results). The standard has also been simplified somewhat with five requirement clauses replacing the extensive 20 criteria listed above (the 20 criteria sit within these five criteria). The requirement clauses are:

1. Quality management system.

2. Management responsibilities.

3. Resource management.

4. Product realization.

5. Measurement, analysis and improvement.

An external auditor for ISO is responsible for assessing a company's operations with respect to the requirement clauses, and only when they are convinced the organization satisfies the criteria will that company be awarded the ISO 9000 accreditation.

Despite the attractions of accreditation, certification and award schemes as a means of auditing companies' quality systems and procedures, there are many critics of such schemes. Some of the main arguments are:

- It is still seen as only an indication, not a guarantee of product or service quality.

- Many organizations are forced or feel obliged to register and receive such awards by their own customers (no registration = no supply).

- The procedures and, in particular, documentation demanded by ISO 9000 is still widely criticized as being overly bureaucratic.

- Does physical existence of documentation and manuals necessarily mean that these procedures are followed?

- Does the outside external auditor readily understand the operations in the organizations he/she visits?

The responsibility and organization for quality

It is widely recognized that accountability for quality cannot be abdicated by any individual working within an organization. A 'total' approach to quality management is now advocated where responsibility for quality is disseminated throughout the organization; at all levels to all departments. A quality system based upon shared responsibility by all individuals and functions provides an effective means of assuring the maintenance and improvement of quality standards.

Despite the need to disperse responsibility for quality throughout the organization, there is still a need to determine how inspection and general quality control activities will be carried out and where these operations will be located. There are many options here, and choices include the incorporation of quality:

- as a department in its own right (unbiased, but risk of isolation);

- within the Production or Operation function (but questions of objectivity and independence from operational pressures?);

- within the Technical function (with a design function, but possibly too insular?).

So although the need for a widespread responsibility for quality throughout a company exists, there still need to be some organizational decisions regarding where the focus of quality management activities should be located. For this reason most organizations still employ a Quality Manager.

Supplier/customer relationship

Incoming quality from suppliers is a crucial factor in determining service and product quality; the relationship between supplier and customer has received much attention over recent years. Over and above material quality, if we are to accept that quality of design is of even greater long-term significance than quality of conformance, then one may appreciate why organizations develop collaborations with suppliers and encourage their participation in new product design programmes. All companies now do this to some extent.

It is important to note that individual organizations are not merely either suppliers or customers: they are both at once. Organizations buy in products and services from others in addition to producing output in the form of goods and services. It is also important to note that a consumer is not merely a person at the end of the overall value chain. All organizations are consumers of the products and services of other organizations. It is imperative that organizations pay attention to supplier/customer relationships and understand that they are both at once. They therefore need to adopt appropriate means of quality control for both the assessment of their own in-house activities and for the assessment of quality of incoming materials and services. These are outlined in rest of this chapter.

Measuring quality

When measuring quality, a distinction can be drawn between the measurement of quality by 'variables' and by 'attributes'. Measurement by variables can occur when quality can be calibrated against scale or in numbers (e.g. dimensional size, weight, speed, number in box, etc.). Measurement by attributes occurs where no scale exists (e.g. a light bulb works or it does not, the judgement of good or poor appearance such as paint finish, etc.).

It is also useful to distinguish between quality measurement activities for the purpose of controlling production and operations processes and the assessment of bought-in materials from an outside supplier. Internal control of processes is most commonly achieved via the measurement of variables, whereas the assessment of incoming materials is most frequently done by attributes.

As stated previously, organizations act as both producers and consumers (of services and/or goods) at the same time. They will, therefore, all be involved with process control and quality inspection of incoming items to varying degrees. So, in additional to organizing the quality system, recognizing and managing the costs of quality and defining responsibilities, they must be aware of the specific techniques that are available for both the control of processes and the assessment of bought-in materials and services.

Statistical Process Control (SPC)

Many forms of quality control exist, but two forms in particular have been extensively used in business organizations to ensure services and products attain and maintain the required standards. These are *statistical process control* or *SPC*, as widely used for the control of processes where measurement is by variables, and *acceptance sampling* where assessment of incoming goods and services to the organizations are assessed on the basis of attributes. Each of these will now be considered.

SPC is used for the quality control of processes by variables and makes use of 'Process Control Charts', as devised in the 1920s by Dr Shewhart of the Bell Telephone Laboratory in the USA. The Shewhart Control Chart indicates when a process is changing (i.e. becoming unstable). The approach is known as statistical process control as it controls a process using the numbers generated by that process. SPC charts can be used for both service and manufacturing processes, for example:

- The time it takes to process anything
  - e.g. scanning items at the supermarket, making paint, order taking.
- The number of defects in individual vehicles as they come off an assembly line.
- The number of straws being supplied to a fast food outlet.
- The level of chlorine in water.
- The percentage of poorly cooked hamburgers.
- The number of supplier/customer complaints per month.
- Etc. . . .

SPC relies upon the measurement of the mean average of variables and their variability around the mean, and assumes

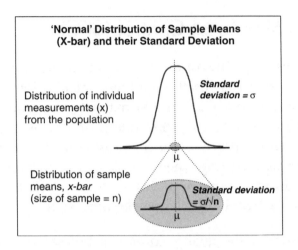

'Normal' Distribution of Sample Means (X-bar) and their Standard Deviation

Distribution of individual measurements (x) from the population

Standard deviation = σ

Distribution of sample means, x-bar (size of sample = n)

Standard deviation = σ/√n

Figure 9.2   Normal distribution

a 'normal' distribution of variables around that mean (see Figure 9.2). The so-called 'normal' distribution is created by collecting over 31 data points and plotting their distribution about their mean. Mathematically this is known as the Central Limit Theory will create 'bell curve' shape, the normal distribution. For example, wooden pencils are produced in a continuous length and chopped to size. If we assume a continuous length of pencil travels down a track and is chopped by a blade at regular intervals we might get some variation in length. If we collect 31 samples or over, measure their lengths and plot the results we will see a normal distribution (bell curve) much like that in Figure 9.2. Remember, over 31 data points and the Central Limit Theorem applies.

However, the bell curve can be different shapes and this can tell us about the reliability of the actual process. Using the example of the pencils, if there is little variation in the measured length the bell curve will be 'tall' and 'skinny' (see Figure 9.3, distribution A): an ideal state. However, if there is great variation in length the curve might more resemble that of distribution C, so-called 'short' and 'fat'. Not an ideal state in terms of process

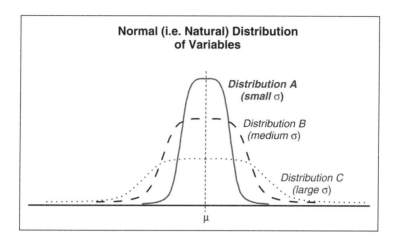

Figure 9.3 Different shape bell curves

control. The consequences of this state are that some pencils may be too long (giving raw material away for free) and some too short (the customer does not receive the length as advertised). This data is useful because with it we can begin to predict the percentage of pencils that are too long or too short. The theory behind this technique also allows us to factor in other issues, such as the range (the difference between the 'smallest' and the 'largest') and the actual tolerance required by the customer, the specification.

Two main forms of charts are used: the average or 'X-Bar' chart which tests for significant changes in sample means, and the range or 'R' chart which tests for significant changes in the spread of variables. The R chart is always used in conjunction with the X-Bar chart. Typical uses in services include: call waiting times in call centres; call dealing times in call centres; processing speed through supermarket checkouts; processing speed through airline check-in desks, etc.

An 'X-Bar' (see Figure 9.4) averages control chart is constructed in the following way:

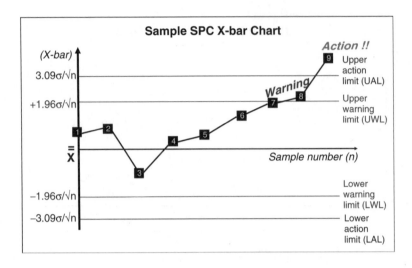

Figure 9.4 X-Bar chart

1. Plot sample number on horizontal axis.

2. Calculate sample mean, X-bar.

3. Calculate and draw in upper and lower action and warning limits.

4. Plot sample averages on vertical axis.

The range chart is especially useful when collecting large data sets from continuous operations. Under these conditions we do not measure and plot every data point; instead 'sets' are grouped together (in fives, tens, etc.) and the average of that group is plotted. This has the advantage of presenting the information in a condensed way. The disadvantage is that by using averages of the data points the actual measurements can become softened or blurred. For instance, see Table 9.1.

Note the averages in the table are the same but the variation in the sample points is substantial. This is highlighted in a range chart (see Figure 9.5).

1. An 'R' range chart is constructed using the method:

Table 9.1   Why are range charts useful?

	Day 1	Day 2
Sample 1	21	16
Sample 2	24	29
Sample 3	22	17
Sample 4	23	28
Sample 5	22	22
Average	22.4	22.4
Range (R)	3	13

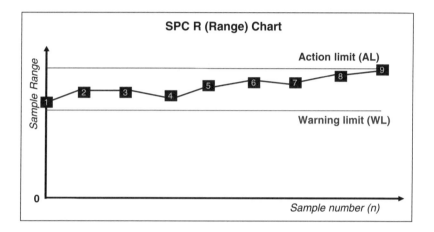

Figure 9.5   R chart

2. Plot sample number.

3. Plot sample number on horizontal axis.

4. Calculate average range (w).

5. Calculate and draw in upper action and warning limits only (since a lower limit would indicate an improvement).

6. Plot sample ranges on vertical axis.

SPC has been popularized by the widespread adoption and introduction of 'Six Sigma' (6σ) within businesses. The phrase six sigma refers to the degree of process control, when a process operates at six sigma the variation is so small that services or products are provided 99.9996 % defect free (or 3.4 defects per million). There is more about this technique in the next chapter.

Acceptance sampling

The batch assessment of incoming materials normally results in one of two basic decisions: reject or accept. One could inspect 100 % of incoming items, but this is costly and very time consuming (e.g. think about supermarkets receiving all the goods during a 24-hour cycle, no time there to inspect). Therefore a sampling approach is normally adopted, commonly known as 'acceptance sampling'. The technique is essentially one of making a decision regarding the 'Acceptable Quality Level' (AQL). This is the proportion of incoming goods in the form of defectives that an organization is willing to accept (could be 1 % or 2 %, etc.). These percentages and the degree of reliability of this method are mathematically calculated.

Summary

The management of quality is a wide-ranging and rather complex issue. On the one hand it could be seen as assuring quality through the use of statistical techniques. This would ensure operations output attains or surpasses pre-identified standards. However, one should not ignore the rather more qualitative aspects when managing quality: the issues of where responsibility for quality lies and how best to organize quality being issues to which we shall return in later chapters. It is also important to note that design of the product or service has a profound effect on its eventual quality: thus modern quality management comprises not just attention upon the conformance to specification, but also ensuring that the said specification of the product or service is correct and appropriate in the first case.

The chapter has also considered the accreditation, certification and award schemes open to organizations from external bodies. These are largely an attempt to increase the standard of quality assurance systems employed by organizations to increase confidence in the quality of incoming goods and services. They also provide vendors with increased confidence in the suppliers they deal with as they are able to discriminate between companies having accreditation (and therefore having passed an external examination) and those who do not. However these schemes do have their critics who see them as an imposition and who question their merit in the light of increasing bureaucracy within many organizations' quality systems.

This chapter also considered the way in which quality is measured and has distinguished between the control of quality where measurement is made by variables and by attributes. It has been noted that producers of goods and services will tend to collate detailed data based upon measurements of variables and the commonly adopted SPC approach to this form of quality control has been presented. From the customer perspective, however, decisions on quality, for example at goods inward inspection, are often based upon attribute data, most commonly either acceptable or unacceptable. Acceptance sampling and the use of attribute charts is commonly used for the quality assurance of incoming goods and services.

Example – Quality Management

'Many organizations quite rightly put a big emphasis on quality management, on quality of design and getting things right first time. However, some organizations underestimate another important component of any quality management programme that is not just the failure prevention, but also failure recovery, actually recovering the situation for the customer.

I travel quite frequently on airlines and have experience of one well known airline, who shall remain nameless for this example, who put a lot of emphasis into quality management. It provides a very good quality service and has an excellent reputation and several national and international awards for quality, but I have observed that when something does go wrong or when there is a problem they can't respond or react to in an appropriate way, they fail in their customer service. So, for example with this particular airline, sometimes there might be problems with the food or the television screen not working in front of the customer. The experience that I had was that, yes, very good service was provided, but when there was a problem suddenly they hadn't got in place the rules and procedures for employees to follow to actually recover the error, i.e., to explain to the customer what has gone wrong and try and put it right or to compensate. Instead they appeared to ignore the situation for as long as possible and only after persistent complaining did they eventually send the most junior member of the team to talk with the customer.

Now, this is a very important area because although we might design for quality and we might try to ensure quality by design, there will inevitably be errors, problems or customer perceptions that view the service as not being up to standard. What is important here is that in these cases we must (a) identify and then (b) respond to these particular situations. So, it is particularly important that we do actually recover errors as and when they occur and in fact if this is done correctly, i.e., you provide a really excellent service and exceed the customer's expectation through your response, you can actually end up with a customer even more delighted with your service than if nothing had gone wrong in the first place!'

Example – Customer Complaint

'The supplier is a global semiconductor manufacturer and the customer is an Italian automotive manufacturer. A product was returned from the customer with ESD or Electro Static Discharge failures. There were no problems reported with this particular product going to other customers, so the evidence from the supplied customers said there were no problems with that particular batch. A visit to the customer in Italy highlighted that the devices were formed by machine and then they were sent along a chute to a collecting bin. The component was then hand assembled into the circuit, the hand assembly stage was fine and all ESD care was taken.

The problem was after the forming by machine, the chute the devices ran down was the type of plastic which generated static electricity. So a simple $2 piece of plastic caused major failures in the application, which they assigned to the supplied component. So here we have a case of the customer reporting a major failure which was actually due to a bad operations process in their assembly. They were very embarrassed.'

Further reading

- Besterfield, D.H. (2008) *Quality Control*, 8th edn, Prentice Hall.

- Dale, B.G. (2008) *Managing Quality*, 5th edn, Wiley Blackwell Publishers Inc.

- Feigenbaum, A.V. (2007) *Total Quality Control*, 4th edn, McGraw-Hill. Garvin, D.A. (1984) What does quality really mean. *Sloan Management Review*, **26**(1), 25–43.

- Shewhart, W. (1980) *Economic Control of Quality of Manufactured Product*, ASQC/Quality Press.

- Slack, N., Chambers, S. and Johnston, R. (2007) *Operations Management*, Prentice Hall: Harlow.

- Wheeler, D.J. (2000) *Understanding Variation: The Key to Managing Chaos*, 2nd edn, SPC Press Inc.

Useful internet sites

- www.asq.org American Society for Quality.

- www.iso.ch International Organization for Standardization (ISO). Details on ISO 9000 and other standards.

- www.qualitydigest.com Quality Digest. Access to magazine, news and tips on quality management.

- www.quality-foundation.co.uk British Quality Foundation.

- www.ukas.com UK Accreditation Service.

Useful academic journal articles

- Deming, W.E. (1985) Transformation of Western-style management. *Interfaces*, 15(3), 6–11.

- Parasuraman, A., Zeithaml, V.A. and Berry, L.L. (1985) A conceptual model of service quality and its implications for future research. *Journal of Marketing*, 49(4), 41–50.

- Parasuraman, A., Zeithaml, V.A. and Berry, L.L. (1988) SERVQUAL: a multiple item scale for measuring consumer perceptions of service quality. *Journal of Retailing*, 64(1), 12–40.

10 IMPROVING THE OPERATIONS

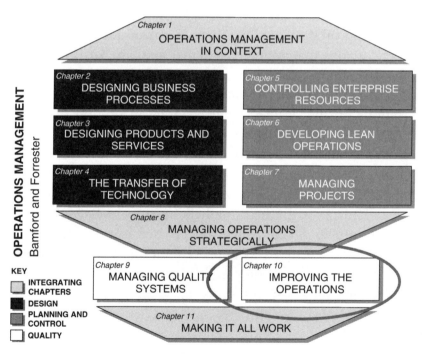

Conceptual model of operations management

Introduction

For the past few decades both academic authors and practitioners have been advocating a wider ranging concept of quality management, and methods for its improvement. Most notable amongst these so-called 'quality gurus' are Deming, Juran, Feigenbaum, Crosby and Taguchi. The basic arguments of each of these are presented in the first part of this chapter. The costs of quality concept is then explored in more detail prior to a detailed description of a range of quality management programmes as employed by both service and production organizations. There then follows an analysis of the quality management concept and philosophy.

It is now recognized that physical inspection and post operations rectification are not enough by themselves to assure service and product quality. There is a need for the design of wider 'quality management systems' and, in particular, specific 'procedures' to ensure quality standards are consistently maintained. A number of 'Standards' exist against which organizations can be certified by an external institution that they conform to a set quality system criteria. The most widely recognized of these is the international standard ISO 9000 (2000) series, as detailed in the previous chapter. Many major purchasing organizations have adopted the ISO 9000 series as a means of standardization for their suppliers, an entry level requirement or order qualifier. Companies are assessed to this standard so they may be registered as approved suppliers. It is now policy within many companies and government departments only to deal with those organizations that are registered under this standard.

Writers on quality management

W. Edwards Deming

Deming (1982; 1986) advocated that quality is management's responsibility and should embrace the philosophy that mistakes and defects are not acceptable. Deming saw quality as being analogous to 'delighting the customer'. Commonly seen as the father of quality control in Japan (where he worked following the Second World War), he argued that employees should be able to report problems without fear of recrimination and that a series of tools, particularly statistical techniques, should be developed to measure and control quality. Deming provided 14 points for ensuring high product quality and customer satisfaction in its broadest sense. These included points such as: ceasing dependence on mass inspection; breaking down barriers between departments; and instituting a vigorous programme of education and training (see Deming, 1982: 17–50).

Joseph Juran

Another pioneer of quality management practice in Japan (where he worked following the Second World War), Juran advocated a trilogy: quality planning; control; and improvement (Juran and Gryna, 1980). He believed that 'annual improvement' through target setting (as in cost budgeting), 'hands on management' and training are fundamental in achieving quality excellence. Juran defined quality as meaning 'fitness for use', and so covered the following areas:

- Quality of Design (design concept and specification).

- Quality of Conformance (match between finished product and its specification).

- Availability (reliability and maintainability in use).

- Safety (risk of injury due to product hazards).

- Field Use (delivery performance, service and condition at point of use).

Juran provided a seven stage 'breakthrough sequence' for quality management. This included: (i) breakthrough in attitudes; (ii) Identify the few vital projects; (iii) organize for breakthrough in knowledge; (iv) conduct the analysis; (v) determine how to overcome resistance to change; (vi) institute the change; (vii) Institute controls (see Juran and Gryna, 1980).

Armand Feigenbaum

Feigenbaum (1983) developed the concept of Total Quality Control (TQC), better known as Total Quality Management (TQM), whereby everyone in the organization shares responsibility for quality and should seek to detect and correct errors and defects at source. Like Deming and Juran, Feigenbaum was an American, although it was the Japanese who first made the total quality concept work at the level of the individual worker.

Kaoru Ishikawa

Ishikawa was influenced by Deming, Juran and Feigenbaum, and is credited with the conception and introduction of the practice of quality circles. He saw the need for all employees, not just a few specialists, to participate in quality improvement and also invented one of the most widely used techniques in quality circles, the 'fishbone' or 'Ishikawa' diagram (see Ishikawa, 1972).

Philip Crosby

Crosby, formerly Vice-President and Director of Quality for ITT, argued it does not cost money to improve quality: rather the benefits of improved quality far outweigh the time and resources spent on its achievement. Crosby advocates a goal of 'Zero Defects' and continual improvement towards this objective. His 14 Point Programme for quality included: management commitment; quality measurement; corrective action; goal setting; and recognition (see Crosby, 1979).

Geniichi Taguchi

Taguchi (1986) developed an approach to quality assurance entitled 'Quality Engineering'. The objective is to design and develop high quality products in a way that reduces costs. Taguchi's methods are in fact highly complex, but involve experiments on the process and statistical analyses, supplemented by interactive team sessions to discuss the data and results. The aim of this is to identify those factors contributing to the product's quality problems and then determining those operations methods and process settings that optimize quality.

Mazaki Imai

Imai's main contribution to the field of quality management was his attempt to identify exactly what the Japanese notion of quality management involved. He argued that in Japan the emphasis is upon constant, incremental and 'never-ending' improvement of quality, what he termed 'kaizen' (Japanese for continuous improvement). Furthermore his book, which is effectively a 'how to do it' handbook, went on to identify 16 components which, together, comprise kaizen within Japanese companies. This included: profit planning; customer satisfaction; just-in-time production; systems improvement; total productive maintenance (TPM); and top management commitment.

He also popularized the use of 5S (Sorting, Straightening, Sweeping, Standardizing, Sustaining), a method for organizing a workplace. The key targets of 5S are workplace morale and efficiency.

Summarizing the writers on quality

Whilst, on the one hand, it can be argued that the writers above have been most influential in spreading the need for quality amongst managers in industry, there are a number of criticisms one can draw in relation to the writers on quality. These include:

1. Many of the writers are extremely prescriptive. There is often a lack of depth to analysis and a lack of theoretical framework to their work. As a result many assumptions are made which may or may not hold for individual organizations.

2. Advocates of quality management often tend to accept what has been said by the quality gurus as 'gospel'. Practicing managers and, in some cases, quality management academics, unquestioningly accepted the views of many of these writers.

3. Some of the writings actually conflict with present-day perceived best practice. For example, a cursory read of Deming displays an assumption of functional organization structures in the way that he suggests departments should see the next upstream department as the customer. Modern day organizations may, in fact, resolve their quality problems more effectively through the adoption of a product-focused or cellular organization structure instead of

developing the supplier-customer relationships advocated by Deming.

The central proactive common theme underlying these works is that quality involves all people in the organization and should not merely be seen as the domain of a specialist quality control department. However management should see itself as ultimately responsible for quality and service to the customer. The above philosophies have greatly shaped the various practices employed by organizations in the management of quality. It is to these practices – the various techniques and programmes – that we turn in the rest of the chapter.

Programmes for quality improvement

Over the last 30 years a number of approaches and group methods have been developed which seek to tackle the wider issues of quality improvement. In keeping with the views of the writers discussed above, the philosophy behind all these approaches is that 'quality is not just nice to have, but essential', 'quality is everyone's responsibility', and that organizations must strive for 'continuous improvement'. For the purposes of this book the 10 quality improvement programmes which merit discussion are zero defects, quality circles, kaizen, quality improvement teams, quality function deployment, value analysis, total quality management, quality costing, business process reengineering and Six Sigma. Note that 'lean' was covered in Chapter 6.

(i) Zero defects

A zero defects (ZD) programme (pioneered by Crosby) aims to reverse the attitude of 'that's good enough' to one that strives for perfection in quality and service: a 'right first time' attitude. The approach recognizes two ways to change attitudes: (i) through product/customer awareness; and (ii) through quality awareness. In ZD the individuals are shown that their own tasks are important. ZD is a campaign based approach and therein lies its drawbacks. There are arguments that the approach: is simplistic; takes no account of individual motivation factors; requires a high degree of cooperation from all; does not tend to infiltrate suppliers; and is rather dated.

(ii) Quality circles

Quality circles are voluntary groups of employees (six to 12 people) who meet on a regular basis and provide a long term focus for improvement. Each group has a leader and meetings tend to follow a formal structure. The overall programme within a company is usually coordinated by a 'facilitator' and there is close liaison with management, to ensure that the problems worked on tie-in with company strategy. The quality circle approach assumes quality conscious employees and usually offers no direct financial incentive to circle members.

Quality circles normally require training in quality matters and problem solving techniques such as brainstorming (free flow idea generation), Pareto (80/20 rule), cause and effect ('fishbone' or 'Ishikawa') diagrams, Statistical Process Control (SPC), etc. At the conclusion of a project, circles normally conduct a formal presentation of recommendations to senior management (the decision makers). Typically, a quality circle project will comprise the following steps:

1. Brainstorm a list of problems and issues.
2. Select project from the list in (1) using Pareto analysis.

3. Represent the problem on a fishbone diagram to illustrate and categorize the main causes.

4. Collect information and analyse.

5. Develop solution.

6. Make recommendations.

The benefits of quality circles are usually defined as:

- Improved employee relations; improved quality; increased motivation/responsibility for quality; employees more receptive to new methods and ideas; provides a forum for discussion/communication.

Quality circles also have a number of problems and issues related to them:

- Senior management commitment is critical to their success; there can be resentment from employees: a feeling that the workforce are doing management's job; frequently there is resentment from managers who see circles as eroding of their prerogatives.

(iii) Kaizen

Imai (1986) used the Japanese for continuous improvement, 'kaizen', to sum-up the approach of Japanese manufacturing companies over the last 30 years in achieving and then maintaining consistently high product and service quality levels. However, use of the term has come to mean something more specific. For example, in the UK kaizen programmes usually involve establishing management initiated corrective action teams comprising individuals who are predominantly not improvement professionals. Kaizen projects tend to run over a concentrated time span, typically a week, and involve the secondment of team members from their normal jobs and duties over this time. This style of improvement is much more like a task force. The emphasis in kaizen is upon 'implementation' and it is usually considered that a project is not complete until the results have been achieved and consistently maintained. So, although the project is a 'one-off' the actual cumulative improvement process is continuous.

(iv) Quality improvement teams

Whereas zero defects, quality circles and kaizen programmes have their own distinctive features, use of the term *quality improvement teams* (QITs) is in wide parlance in service and manufacturing organizations. In essence it is a very general term which covers a range of different small group quality improvement activities; these can be anything from a totally voluntary quality circle team approach to a relatively highly structured, mandatory and management initiated kaizen programme. The QIT term and others like it (e.g. error-cause removal teams, continuous improvement groups, process improvement groups, etc.) have become popular because they enable managers to detach their quality improvement programmes from labels such as ZD, quality circles and kaizen which have, in some cases, received bad press and have poor perceptions in the minds of the general public and trade union organizations. The other benefit is the degree of 'tailoring' that can be done to ensure a better fit between the improvement methodology chosen and the organization's culture.

(v) Quality Function Deployment (QFD)

QFD is a process which brings together and analyses the essential elements and important characteristics of the phases in the product/service life cycle (introduction, growth, maturity, decline) from its conception through design, development, production, distribution, use and, finally, termination. It focuses and coordinates skills within the organization and encourages teamwork between personnel from different functional areas within the business. By recognizing the interrelationships between the design/engineering properties of the product/service and the customers' requirements, appropriate actions can be taken at every stage of the life cycle so that customer needs are effectively anticipated, prioritized and incorporated into the product or service. See Chapter 3.

(vi) Value analysis

Value analysis was introduced previously under product design. It is also closely associated with the continuous improvement of products (and processes) as it seeks to increase customer satisfaction from existing resources through the adoption of teamwork within the organization. See Chapter 3.

(vii) Total Quality Management (TQM)

TQM was developed from the lessons learned from Japanese organizations. It is a broad philosophy and applied process of implementing a formalized structure of management education and activities for dealing with quality issues. It is based on the assumption that the majority of quality issues can be handled by focused management activity, leading to improved quality of work and greater levels of quality in the whole organization. This will in turn lead to higher levels of distinctive quality at an acceptable and competitive cost.

TQM as a philosophy of quality has been summarized as: 'Quality equals delighting the customer'. The distinctive approach of TQM can be summarized as comprising seven basic principles:

1. *The Approach* = Management-led

2. *The Scope* = Company-wide

3. *The Scale* = Everyone is responsible

4. *The Philosophy* = Prevention not detection

5. *The Standard* = Right-first-time

6. *The Control* = Cost of quality

7. *The Theme* = Continuous improvement

TQM was an extremely popular concept and has been afforded considerable attention in the media and academic journals. There are, however, two fields of thought. The first has a positive view of TQM: one that sees its adoption as the saviour of many laggard companies in the West who have learned from Japanese practice. The second camp has a more critical perspective on TQM:

- What comprised TQM varied considerably between different organizations. It was often difficult to link causes with effects when assessing the success of some organizations.

- The comparative ease with which some companies claimed to have changed their organization cultures can be questioned. Culture runs deeper than attitudes: it relates to the underlying assumptions, beliefs and values of people within the organization that have been built up, in some cases, over many decades. It is argued that TQM only changed attitudes and unless considerable effort was made by senior managers, the underlying culture within the organization will revert to type, particularly when faced by external challenges.

- If one accepts that TQM was an umbrella term and that, in practice, its implementation involved the introduction of various quality improvement programmes (as detailed above), then many of the arguments made above also hold for TQM. These criticisms centred around creating a veneer of customer focus and increased industrial democracy, but often the underlying motivation was for managers to increase their relative power over workers and trade unions. This explains why, despite the fact that it is difficult to argue against the value of increasing quality, service and customer focus, many people within organizations and their trade union representatives were sceptical as to the motives of managers in introducing TQM.

(viii) Costs of quality

In the field of quality management there has been considerable attention paid to the quantification of quality in order to judge the benefits and costs that might accrue from alternative courses of action and approaches. In Chapter 9 we considered the use of statistics in the control of quality, but this in itself bears little relation to the broader business objectives of an organization. Following largely on the work of Philip Crosby the idea of costing quality has provided an approach which enables the analysis of quality matters in relation to their financial impact upon the organization.

Quality is a desirable and essential attribute of services and products. It is useful, therefore, to identify the areas where a company would incur penalties (costs of quality) were it not for the quality assurance system. These can be categorized as follows:

1. Quality costs at the design stage: ensuring the right balance between design 'precision' and operational feasibility, e.g.

tolerances not set too tightly as to be impossible to achieve – usually contained within the category of 'costs of prevention'.

2. Quality Costs of Conformance associated with:
   - internal failure (e.g. scrap, rework);
   - external failure (e.g. repair, complaints, returns);
   - appraisal (e.g. inspection, checking, testing, audit, vendor rating);
   - prevention (e.g. planning, materials inspection, training).

So, if we consider quality of design to constitute prevention costs, there are essentially four types of quality cost: internal failure, external failure, appraisal and prevention. Needless to say, these costs of quality must be carefully managed to ensure the cost-effectiveness of the quality system to the business as a whole. Increasing costs of quality for one category can result in reduced costs of another category of quality costs. The key, therefore, is in maintaining the correct balance between the different categories of cost so as to minimize overall costs of quality.

Prevention Costs – costs of planning for quality

- Salaries and development costs for new product or service design.
- Reliability studies and new process equipment design.
- Costs of prototyping and of rigorously testing product performance.
- The analysis of processes to improve performance and the implementation of process control plans (e.g. SPC, acceptance sampling, etc.).
- Developing and operating formal training programmes.
- Etc.

Appraisal Costs – testing and inspection costs (incoming goods, work in progress and finished goods)

- Salaries for inspectors, supervisors and cost of equipment.
- Maintaining instruments (calibration of gauges, etc.).
- Personnel gathering information and analysing quality measurements.

Failure Costs – Two types

(i) **Internal failure costs**:

- Scrap and rework costs (labour, material, overhead costs).
- Corrective action (the error rectification costs from time spent determining the causes of failure and in correcting production or service problems).
- Downgrading costs (including the lost revenue resulting from selling a service or product at a lower price because it does not meet specifications).

(ii) **External failure costs for an organization include:**

- Costs of customer complaints and returns (investigating complaints and taking corrective action).
- Product recall costs (administration and direct costs of making adjustments to faulty products from the field).
- Warranty claims costs (the costs of repair or replacement of products under warranty).
- Product liability costs (the costs of the defence in legal actions and in settlements can, if the organization is not careful, be seen as external failure costs).

It has been estimated by Crosby that 60–90 % of an organization's total cost of quality was in the form of internal and external failure costs. It was assumed that managers could not easily control or influence such variations in quality: they were an accepted fact of business life. Traditionally, the typical reaction of managers to high failure costs was to increase inspection, thereby increasing appraisal costs. Failure costs would then fall but appraisal costs would rise, thereby creating minimal improvement in quality at source or indeed in the profitability. It is now recognized that to improve quality and profitability companies must concentrate on quality assurance by design, and hence consider investing more heavily in prevention. In practice organizations have realized that an increase in the costs of prevention will have large benefits downstream in reduced appraisal and failure costs, thereby reducing total costs of quality (see Figure 10.1).

Therefore many organizations have concerned themselves with measuring and recording their costs of quality in financial terms, and then tracking the effects of actions such as increasing or reducing expenditure in each cost category to observe the impact on overall costs of quality and, hence, profitability. In so doing they hope to reach a lower level of costs through achieving a

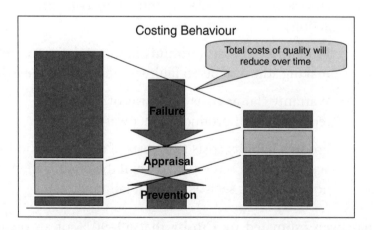

Figure 10.1 Quality costing behaviour

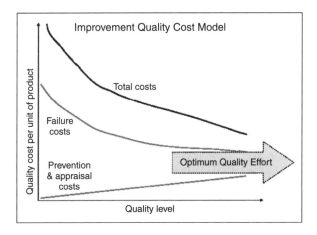

Figure 10.2 Optimal quality costs

near to optimal balance between the different cost of quality categories (see Figure 10.2).

Costing quality, both in terms of prevention and also assigning values to 'non-conformances', provides a way of linking decisions concerning where emphasis should be placed in quality management to the business needs (i.e. profitability) of the business. However costing quality does present some problems:

1. It is often impossible to assign exact and accurate values to the costs of quality. Figures for the costs of quality are, therefore, at best only estimates and, at worst open to considerable doubt.

2. What items should be incorporated in each category of costs? For example, what proportion of research and development (R&D) costs should be apportioned to costs of prevention? And should the lost revenue and opportunity costs of poor reputation resulting from external product failures be included in the failure costs? Again, if so, then how can this be calculated?

(ix) Business process re-engineering (BPR)

BPR reviews all aspects of people, process, technology and organization in a single coordinated approach. Hence, BPR becomes much greater than the sum of its parts. It differs in several ways from more traditional improvement programmes like downsizing, restructuring, rightsizing, total quality management (TQM) or automation. BPR first seeks performance breakthroughs, that is to say radical and discontinuous improvements rather than incremental improvements. Second, BPR pursues multi-faceted improvement goals which include quality, cost, flexibility, speed and accuracy concurrently, while the other programmes focus on fewer goals, or trade off among them. Finally, BPR adopts a process perspective of the business, while the others generally retain a functional or organizational perspective. By its very nature, BPR is a top-down exercise. Since business processes are usually cross-functional and cross-organizational, changes must be authorized at a sufficiently high level in the company.

Hammer (1990), one of the founders of the BPR approach, defines the technique as *'the fundamental rethinking and radical redesign of business processes to achieve dramatic improvements in critical contemporary measures of performance such as cost, quality, service and speed'*. Before Hammer packaged the theory attractively for managers, it had been floating round US academia since 1983. Eight major stages are involved:

Stage 1: Identify the need for reengineering and business vision.

Stage 2: Obtain the business unit leader's commitment.

Stage 3: Identify process to be redesigned.

Stage 4: Understand and measure existing processes.

Stage 5: Identify the enabling role of IT and design new process.

Stage 6: Specify the technical and social solutions.

Stage 7: Transform the business processes.

Stage 8: Continuous process improvement.

BPR was extremely popular amongst senior executives. It appeared to provide a logical and rational way to develop product and customer focused organizations in order to improve business performance and increase quality and service levels. However, a considerable backlash emerged against BPR:

- BPR signalled a return to scientific management as propounded by Frederick Taylor. It considered the organization as a set of mechanisms (business processes) which could be 'engineered' and primed for maximum efficiency. The approach takes little or no account of the human issues in organizational design.

- BPR equals 'downsizing': another gimmick employed by management to exert power, influence and remove labour from the operations process wherever necessary.

- The results very short term. The dehumanizing effect of BPR resulted in the underperformance of some of the publicized success story companies in the longer term.

(x) Six sigma

Six sigma (6σ) is, according to Juran, '*A data-driven process-improvement methodology*'. It is a statistical concept that tracks the amount of variation in a process relative to the set specification or customer requirement. When a process operates at six sigma the variation is so small that services or products are provided 99.9996 % defect free (or 3.4 defects per million, Figure 10.3). This is called 'World Class' for most organizations. Employing six sigma involves extensive specialist training

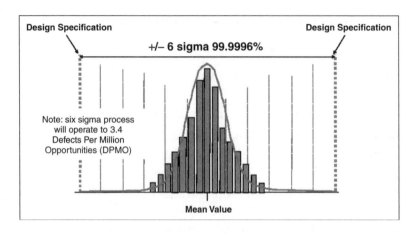

Figure 10.3 Six sigma (6σ) process capability

of key personnel; they become certified practitioners (holding various coloured belts to indicate their level of training and experience in application: Green, Black, and Master Black Belt). In terms of the company infrastructure needed to deploy and support it, the organization must have the 'right' quality environment/culture/system in place to become a 'six sigma company'. The implementation of six sigma requires: a six sigma champion; careful project selection; a project sponsor; a Master Black Belt; other Black Belts on the team; a project team: Green Belts (often as part of training) and others.

But who is using it and why? From early 1986 Motorola and then General Electric (GE) have implemented it into their operations processes and claim major multi-million dollar savings. Six sigma is very popular and is being used 'politically' within many organizations, to demonstrate senior management's commitment to improvement both internally and to external stakeholders. Various consulting organizations offer attractive training packages and its use has moved outside traditional manufacturing into the service industry, including healthcare providers.

But is it an improvement method or a philosophy to be adopted? Some say it is merely a repackaging of TQM and the other quality tools. Indeed recently there has been a surge in tailored improvement initiatives, such as 'lean six sigma' approaches). Six sigma does provide a useful guide for a logical progression through problem solving and in directing when and which tools to use. One formal taught approach is DMAIC: define, measure, analyse, improve, control. A criticism which most practitioners agree upon is that it provides little attention to the 'soft' issues (i.e. the people).

Criticisms of quality improvement programmes

Some criticisms of the various quality improvement programmes adopted by organizations over past decades have been covered in the subsections above. However some general points for discussion and debate can be raised:

1. Many of the programmes assume the existence of a compliant and pliable workforce. Perhaps the reason for the success of some of these programmes is because most workers and trade unions in the West have reduced powers of defiance due to economic circumstances and industrial action legislation. Under such circumstances, to what extent have employees actually taken quality improvement in the form of these programmes truly to their hearts?

2. To what extent are these programmes window dressing in the interests of positive publicity and customer relations by senior managers? To what extent are they an attempt to cover over existing and perennial problems within the organization?

3. Many of these programmes present a threat to conventional management–trade union negotiations; are we truly content to see direct individual relationships between workers and managers replace collective bargaining in the workplace?

4. It is often difficult for individuals to complain about the imposition of these programmes because of the risk of appearing 'anti-quality'. Most people are 'pro-quality' in principle, but should there be more open debate as to the ways and means of achieving optimal quality levels in place of the imposition of new quality initiatives so often foisted on the workforce by over-zealous managers?

This section has summarized a wide range of quality improvement programmes introduced by managers. No single programme is a panacea to solve all problems. Rather an organization must select those programmes which seem most suited to their own circumstances, whilst guarding against launching so many new initiatives as to confuse its employees. To succeed, the concept of quality improvement programmes becoming a 'flavour of the month' must be avoided at all cost. The key to this is long term senior management commitment.

Quality award schemes

A number of award schemes for companies displaying 'excellence' in quality management exist to recognize and publicize best practice. To an extent these schemes can serve the same purpose as formal quality improvement programmes; in theory they unite a company around a central idea or concept and provide a degree of improvement focus for the business. In this case with an external view. Well known award schemes range from the Deming Application Prize; the Malcolm Baldrige National Quality Award (MBNQA) and the European Quality

Award (EQA); to national and regional awards within various countries. Probably the most well known award world-wide is the US Baldridge Award whereby each year companies enter and are assessed on a marking scheme for their quality systems, product quality, customer service, etc. The highest scorers receive an award in recognition of their performance and excellence. The European Union introduced a similar scheme exclusively for companies operating in Europe; the European Foundation for Quality Management (EFQM) operates the European Quality Award, using their 'Excellence Model' to provide the framework for assessing organizations (see Figure 10.4).

Claimed benefits of quality awards include: structured approach; identified strengths and areas for improvement; helps management understand TQM; helps develop, manage and integrate improvement activities; enables progress to be measured and recognized; identifies best practice. According to Richie and Dale (1999) difficulties experienced with quality awards include: lack of commitment and enthusiasm; time consuming nature of the

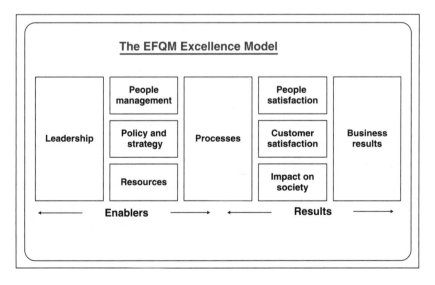

Figure 10.4 EFQM excellence model

process; not knowing where to start; selling the concept to staff; people not realizing the need for documented evidence; lack of cross-functional integration; assessment done in time to link to business plans.

Many organizations now see such award schemes as an important part of their quality initiative: receipt of an award is taken as a useful benchmark in comparison with other companies and helps to publicize the company as 'excellent' with regard to quality and service.

Summary

This chapter has presented improvement as a holistic philosophy which, if one had to summarize in a phrase, entails the introduction of programmes to increase the customer focus and quality awareness of individuals and groups within an organization. The chapter took a tour through the main writers on quality from the past few decades and introduced the concept of cost of quality. A number of so-called 'programmes' for improvement were presented and a section was incorporated which detailed criticism against many of these. Finally, quality award schemes were briefly presented. As a concluding thought, how should organizations improve their operations? Appropriately! Organizations need to take into account the 'environmental' conditions under which they operate: changing legislation, stakeholder demands, economic instability and breakdown in some countries, etc. These must all be factored into and balanced with any improvement methodology adopted; as should the overriding strategy that the company is employing. Whatever improvements are made they *must* fit with the current and projected trajectory of the firm.

Example – Quality Circles

'The company is a carpet manufacturer, very high quality. The emphasis is very much on a quality product, and I think that is the first important thing you need to have, a culture, indeed an ethos, within the company that is supportive of quality. You can't just introduce a quality programme and expect everybody to participate from day one; you need a culture and an organization that is conducive to accepting quality and the need for quality improvement.

The company is family owned, over many generations, with very little labour turnover and lots of skills in the business. But this didn't mean that quality improvement would succeed. You have to be prepared that only 10 to 15 % of people will volunteer to participate and there is a real need for training and facilitation. So a key part in any quality programme is to employ someone full time who would be involved in training people. To demonstrate brainstorming techniques, how to run meetings, pro rata type analyses to identify important projects; and not least of all data collection, presentation of solutions and most importantly of all, implementation. So a lot of emphasis in quality needs to go on training and development, particularly when a new quality programme has just been started and needs to be led through the first few crucial weeks.

So this is really an example of a company that has continued to be successful over many years and is still profitable in a very difficult industry. It has brought its people on board in terms of tackling quality and showing quality is important. This was done not just in terms of its words but through its actions, through its provision of training and development through formal quality programmes.'

Example – Continuous improvement

'This is an international coffee company. Senior management identified issues with the way that Paninis were "processed", how we actually cooked them and got them to the customer as an end product. We were actually having a lot of problems throughout the UK, especially in stores where we had very, very high volumes.

We thought some fresh, blue sky thinking, would help, so we looked at ways to improve and change the process. We actually looked step-by-step at the process: what was going on at the cash register and the putting of the Panini on the grill and then where the problems came about, what the different end problems were. So we had Paninis that were coming out charred, with cheese going everywhere, these didn't look attractive as a product; and we had customers who didn't know what filling was inside because it had so much cheese leaking out. As a result we sometimes had vegetarians taking meat Paninis away. We often ended up with a whole backlog of issues at the counter and the cash register. This was very stressful for both the staff and the customers!

So we looked at what the problems were, where the process was going wrong, where it was breaking down, and we looked at a whole range of solutions that could solve the different problems. The simplest solutions are often the best, as was the case here. After trying many scenarios we chose one which we felt would actually change everything, having somebody responsible for ensuring the Paninis were *put on the grill and removed at the right time. So we have a tag system now and make sure that the coffee tag says what the coffee was and also which Panini went with it. Actually we have an extra box on it too, so that at the end you go to the customer and say, "this is your coffee and it goes with this Panini", and to make sure that there is eye contact, to make sure that the Panini had registered and was in fact the correct Panini. Problem solved!'*

Example – Kaizen

'This is an event that we ran in our new packaging area. The idea sprang from the opportunity that was clear to us from our KPI (key performance indicator) measurements; we were taking three hours to change over a particular piece of equipment which was far too long. We called in an external kaizen expert who ran an event for us and we pulled together a multi-functional team including engineers, electricians, operators and the engineering manager. We also included the team leader for the area. During the week what the team did was looked at this process as a kaizen exercise, so they were identifying wastes and looking for opportunities to eliminate those wastes, and those wastes were movement, weighting, etc.

By the end of the week, the ideas that had been generated, and they had been generated from all levels, including the operators most impressively, had given us the opportunity to reduce the change over time by 50%. So our change over time was now one and a half hours instead of three hours, which is a pretty impressive result. The learn from this is that there is a lot of intellectual resource out there, in the factory, that we just haven't been using. We learnt a lot from that and have since run many minor kaizen events ourselves and made similar improvements.'

Example – 5S

'We want to make sure that everybody on site understands the 5S, understands what it means and understands that it is more than just picking up a brush and sweeping up. Now when we trained all the associates we had a bit of theory to tell them about 5S and what it means but then we used a practical exercise to demonstrate it.

We had a big box with a jigsaw in. The jigsaw was broken up and we also had lots of "extra" stuff in there, old coins, paper and cups, etc., but no pictures, no diagram to go with that particular jigsaw. We wanted the team to build that jigsaw and they took about ten minutes, then we asked them for continuous improvement ideas and how they could improve how to build the jigsaw.

They came up with lots of useful ideas, i.e., they needed a picture or diagram to work from; that the unnecessary "stuff" should be removed; that the layout of the area they were using could be changed to make access easier; how to sequence the build; and that within the team of five, instead of all doing the jigsaw, to decide in advance who would build what section. They linked it to roles and responsibility.

So then we actually gave them a jigsaw with the improvements they had suggested and they took the build time from nine minutes to one minute.

The key things they understood from this were how 5S can improve both environment and efficiency, and that it improves the actual visual aspect of the plant. This is important to us as we have a high number of customers coming to our plant, more than any other car manufacturer in the world.'

Further reading

- Crosby, P.B. (1979) *Quality is Free*, McGraw-Hill, New York.

- Crosby, P.B. (1996) *Quality is Still Free: Making Quality Certain in Uncertain Times*, McGraw-Hill, New York.

- Dale, B.G. (2008) *Managing Quality*, 5th edn, Wiley Blackwell Publishers Inc.

- Deming, W.E. (1982) *Quality, Productivity and Competitive Position*, MIT Press.

- Deming, W.E. (1986) *Out of the Crisis*, MIT Press.

- Feigenbaum, A.V. (1983) *Total Quality Control: Engineering and Management*, McGraw-Hill.

- Hammer, M. and Champy, J. (1993) *Re-engineering the Corporation: A Manifesto/or Business Revolution*, Harper Business, New York.

- Imai, M. (1986) Kaizen: *The Key to Japan's Competitive Success*, McGraw-Hill.

- Ishikawa, K. (1972) *Guide to Quality Control*, Asian Productivity Press, Tokyo.

- Juran, J.M. (2001) *Juran's Quality Handbook*, 5th edn, McGraw-Hill.

- Juran, J.M. and Gryna, F. (1980) *Quality Planning and Analysis*, McGraw-Hill, New York.

- Kaplan, R.S. and Norton, D.P. (1996) *Balanced Scorecard: Translating Strategy into Action*, Harvard Business School Press, Boston.

- Kaplan, R.S. and Norton, D.P. (2006) *Alignment*, Harvard Business School Press.

- Oakland, J. (1989) *Total Quality Management,* Butterworth-Heinemann, Oxford.

- Oakland, J. (2003) *TQM: Text with Cases,* 2d edn, Butterworth-Heinemann.

- Shingo, S. (1985) *A Revolution in Manufacturing,* Productivity Press, New York.

- Shingo, S. (2008) *Kaizen and the Art of Creative Thinking,* Norman Bodek.

- Taguchi, G., Chowdhury, S. and Wu, Y. (2005) Taguchi *Quality Engineering Handbook,* John Wiley & Sons, Inc.

- Taguchi, G.M. (1986) *Introduction to Quality Engineering,* Asian Productivity Press, Tokyo.

Useful internet sites

- www.apqc.org American Productivity and Quality Centre.

- www.kaizen.com Kaizen Institute.

- www.baldrige.nist.gov National Institute of Standards and Technology (details of the Baldrige Award).

- www.efqm.org European Foundation for Quality Management. Details of the European Quality Award.

- www.qfdi.org QFD Institute.

Useful academic journal articles

- Bamford. D. and Greatbanks R. (2005) The use of quality management tools and techniques: a study of application in everyday situations, *International Journal of Quality and Reliability Management*, **22**(4), 376–92.

- Bamford. D and Xystouri. T. (2005) A case study of service failure and recovery within an international airline, *Managing Service Quality*, **15**(3), 306–22.

11 MAKING IT ALL WORK!

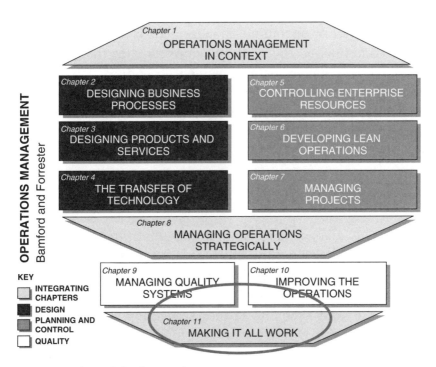

Conceptual model of operations management

Introduction

We have suggested that operations management comprises three essential components:

1. *design of operations* processes, products and services, and the work of individuals;

2. *planning and control* of operations once designs are in place and operational; and

3. ensuring *quality* of products and services produced and delivered, and (wherever possible) improving on these.

But these cannot be addressed in isolation. The essential element in *effective* operations management is the *integration* of these components. The book therefore contains three integrating chapters: operations management in context (Chapter 1); managing operations strategically (Chapter 8); and this chapter, making it all work. This brief chapter provides a summary of the topic of operations management.

Making it all work

Operations management is all about supporting the business and delivering against the business strategy. The contribution of the operations part of the business is often key because it delivers the 'transformation'. The operations function tangibly adds value and therefore creates something that people are willing to pay for. How effectively the function performs this role will, in the short term, determine how profitable the business is. The long term impact of operations can greatly influence the survivability of the business; and whether it can adapt to a changing 'environment' and then recognize and maximize opportunities as they arise.

The operations strategy must support the organization's business strategy and a useful example is that of driving a car. When driving one must constantly look far ahead, to the middle ground, and to the immediately surroundings. As a cycle this is done very quickly and provides essential data as to the future (what is on the road ahead). The important element is then the translation of this 'data' into useful 'information' with which decisions can be made. This will ultimately determine the driver's response and action. The same is true of the operations function, which can provide this 'translation' of data into 'information' for the business. See Figure 11.1.

Operations management concerns the *design* of the service or product, the *control* of the resources, the developed *strategy*, and *systematic* improvement.

Of course, in the twenty-first century we also have new challenges to take into account: quality of working life issues; an ageing population; employment law; business ethics and environmental responsibility; and sustainability, etc. These all impact what is possible as regards operational solutions. The most efficient answer to an operational or business problem may not always be feasible.

Figure 11.1   Continual contribution of operations

Summary

The task of the Operations Manager can be summarized at a basic level as converting a range of resource inputs, through the operations process, into a range of outputs in the form of products. However, the various elements that together make up this management function are diverse and complex in nature. The operations manager must have competencies in human resource management, strategic awareness, product knowledge, systems and organizational design and, at the operating level, of planning and control. Moreover, the task of the operations manager is frequently misunderstood and often relegated to a reactive rather than proactive role within the organization. This is a mistake. As this book has demonstrated, through the application of proven operational tools and techniques the function has a tangible contribution to make to the emergent strategies and initiatives of any business.

Example – The Challenge of Operations

'I want to emphasize the operations challenge from my perspective. We have a one hundred million turnover per year and the challenge for me as a manufacturing manager is that I find myself at the middle level of our business. On the one hand the Executive Team and Board of the business want to see the benefits of lean manufacturing techniques; on the other hand I am constantly battling with them to get the resources to be able to fund a team to deliver those results. This is a constant struggle, because on the one hand we want the results, on the other hand we need to save costs and to reduce the cost of sale. It's a continuous battle!'

SELECTED REFERENCES

Atkinson, J. (1984) Manpower Strategies for Flexible Organizations, *Personnel Management*, August.

Bennett, D.J. and Forrester, P.L. (1993) *Market-Focused Production Systems: Design and Implementation*, Prentice-Hall, Hemel Hempstead.

Bowenkamp, R.D. and Kleiner, B.H. (1987) How to be a Successful Project Manager, *Industrial Management and Data Systems*, 87(3/4).

Burns, T. and Stalker, G.M. (1966) *The Management of Innovation*, Tavistock Publications, London.

Deming, W.E. (1982) *Quality, Productivity and Competitive Position*, MIT Press.

Department of Trade and Industry (DTI) (1988) *Competitive Manufacturing: A Practical Guide to the Development of a Manufacturing Strategy*, IFS Publications, UK.

Duckworth, W.E., Gear, A.E. and Lockett, A.G. (1977) *A Guide to Operational Research*, Chapman and Hall, London.

Gyllenhammar, P. (1977) *People at Work*, Addison-Wesley, Wokingham, UK.

Hammer, M. (1990) Reengineering Work: Don't Automate, Obliterate, *Harvard Business Review* **70**(4).

Hayes, R.H. and Wheelwright, S.C. (1984) *Restoring Our Competitive Edge: Competing Through Manufacturing*, John Wiley & Sons, Inc., New York.

Herzberg, F. (1966) *Work and the Nature of Man*, World Publishing Company, New York.

Hill, T.J. (1985) Manufacturing Strategy: *The Strategic Management of the Manufacturing Function*, Palgrave Macmillan, London

Hill, T.J. (1991) *Production/Operations Management: Text and Cases*, Prentice Hall, Hemel Hempstead.

Hill, T.J. (1993) *Manufacturing Strategy: The Strategic Management of the Manufacturing Function* (2nd edn), Macmillan, London.

Maslow, A.H. (1943) A Theory of Human Motivation, *Psychological Review*, Vol. 50.

McGregor, D.M. (1960) *The Human Side of Enterprise*, McGraw-Hill, New York.

Oakley, M. (1984) *Managing Product Design*, Littlehampton Book Services Ltd, UK.

Porter, M.E. (1985) *Competitive Advantage: Creating and Maintaining Superior Performance*, Free Press.

Roethlisberger, F.J. and Dickson, W.J. (1939) *Management and the Worker*, Harvard University Press, Boston.

Schonberger, R.J. (1986) *World Class Manufacturing: The Lessons of Simplicity Applied*, Free Press, New York.

Skinner, W. (1985) *Manufacturing: The Formidable Competitive Weapon*, John Wiley & Sons, Inc., New York.

Utterbeck, J. and Abernathy, W.J. (1975) A Dynamic Model of Process and Product Innovation, *OMEGA*, Vol. 3, No. 6, pp. 639–656.

Womack, J., Jones, D. and Roos, D. (1990) *The Machine That Changed The World*, Harper Paperbacks, London.

Index

Index